F^5=Grace: A Formula for a E
By: Schenida Lynn Cain Waters

~Acknowledgments~

First, I would like to thank God who once again has given me the opportunity to do HIS will. Secondly, I would like to thank my family and friends who have impacted my life in such a profound manner.

~The Dedication~

This book is dedicated to GOD because everything I do, should be for HIS glory!!!

~Disclaimer~

The writer of this book does not claim to have any special training or expertise on the topics discussed in this book but believes strongly to be led by the spirit while sharing God's word and His revelations.

This book has been formatted with justified margins to form polished margins, which accounts for the extra spaces in between some of the text

Copyright © 2024 by Schenida L.C. Waters

All rights reserved. Except as permitted under the U.S. Copyright Act of 1976, no part of this publication may be reproduced, distributed, or transmitted in any form or by any means, or stored in a database or retrieval system, without the prior written permission of the publisher.

Table of Contents

~

I. Acknowledgments, Dedication, Disclaimer (Page 1)

II. Table of Contents (Page 2)

III. Introduction (Pages 3-6)

IV. God's Grace is AMAZING (Pages 7-12)

V. F^1 = FAMILY: God Blesses The Family (Pages 13-135)

> Roles in the Family:
> Wife (pp. 15-24), Husband (pp. 25-29), Father (pp. 30-36),
> Mother (pp. 37-53), Son (pp. 54-62), Daughter (pp. 63-70), Brother (pp. 71-78),
> Sister (pp. 79-86), Brothers and Sisters in Christ (P. 87-89), Father-in-law (pp. 90-91),
> Mother-in-law (pp. 92-94), Son-in-law (pp. 95-98), Daughter-in-law (pp. 99-101),
> Brother-in-law (pp. 102-104), Sister-in-law (pp. 105-107) Grandmother (pp. 108-110),
> Grandfather (pp. 111-113, Aunt (pp. 114-120), Uncle (pp. 121-122), Cousin (pp. 123-125),
> Nephew (pp. 126-129), Niece (pp. 130-132), Granddaughter (pp. 133-134), Grandson (pp. 135-136),
> Grandchildren (pp. 137-138)

VI. F^2 = FAITH: God Blesses Our Faith (Pages 139-158)

VII. F^3 = FRIENDS: God Blesses Our Friendships (Pages 159-172)

VIII. F^4 = FELLOWSHIPS: God Blesses Our Fellowships (Pages 173-178)

IX. F^5 = FINANCES: God Blesses Our Finances (Pages 179-189)

X. Bibliography and About the Writer (Pages 190)

Title: F⁵=Grace: A Formula for a Blessed Life

Author: Schenida Lynn Cain Waters

~Introduction~

July 22, 2019-Journal Entry:

In the summer of 2017, I volunteered to teach/assist with Vacation Bible School (VBS) at my local church. At the end of the week, I received an unexpected gift from the VBS coordinator. It was a 4-plate display stand home décor item. Each plate had a word: (Family, Faith, Friends, and Fellowship).

I really liked it because of the words and the colors blended well with my colors on my sunporch.

One day I was spending time in solitude on the sunporch, and I was asking the Lord if HE wanted me to write another book.

~Introduction~

I was drawn to the words from the plate décor. I asked God to confirm that I would write a book about the F-words.

Fast forward from 2017 to now (2019) and I was in solitude again after my workout on the sunporch and I was drawn again to the F-words on the plate décor. At that moment, God spoke into my spirit to add another word to make a 5th word (Finances) to the F-words.

I questioned adding another F-word and His spirit said "GRACE."

I remember researching the number five and it means grace. I began thinking about the title of the new book and it was confirmed as "F^5=GRACE: A Formula for a Blessed Life". I read in the New Living Translation commentary once that there is no "Magic Formula" for a blessed life. Our lives are blessed because of God's Grace!

~Introduction~

Each summer, I try to set aside time to fast and pray for the upcoming school year (i.e., grace to begin and finish the year, new students, new parents, teammates, cohorts, custodians, leaders (Principal and Assistant Principals), cafeteria workers, support staff, bus drivers, etc.).

The summer had winded down to seven (7) days left. The spirit spoke to me and said, my grace is sufficient, now fast for five (5) days: July 22 through July 26.

I thought, WOW, how gracious of you God. I had been invited to two (2) events planned for July 27th and 28th which included food. I had thought about a seven (7) day fast with just fruits and veggies but that was my plan. I have been asking God to remind me when I am doing things my way and HE has done just that.

Our wills and brains will take over in a heartbeat.

~Introduction~

So, there I was in solitude again on the sunporch (my favorite place in the house) writing this journal entry and beginning my study on "GRACE" for the introduction of this book. What is grace? The New Living Translation definition is "God's free and unmerited (can't work for) favor toward sinful humanity. The following verses have been summarized based on the New Living Translation.

GOD'S GRACE IS AMAZING!!!

These verses will explain how God is GRACIOUS to US!

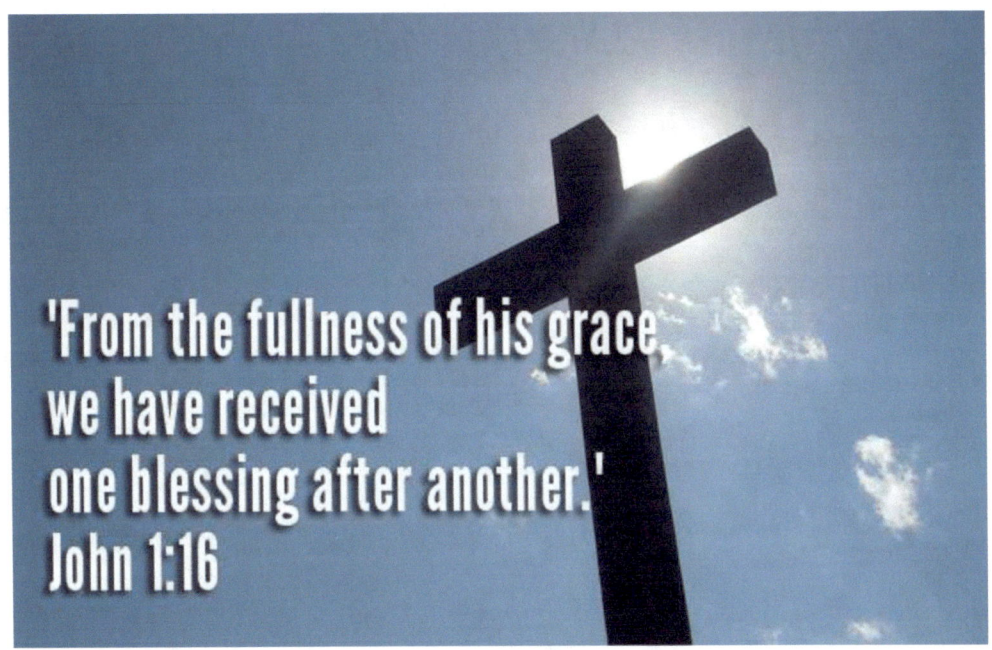

https://dwellingintheword.wordpress.com/wp-content/uploads/2014/04/gj1-cross.jpg

The Lord gives grace and glory and will withhold no good thing from those who walk upright. (Psalm 84:11) We can do God's work only by HIS spirit, not our own strength. Nothing can stand in the way of us finishing God's work and HE gives us grace from start to finish. (Zechariah 4:6-7) God placed His special favor (grace) upon Jesus as He grew strong in spirit and was filled with wisdom. (Luke 2:40)

GOD'S GRACE IS AMAZING!!!

Paul knew that he had become an apostle not by how hard he worked or how zealous he was but only by God's grace. (1 Corinthians 15:10) We are saved by grace (Acts 15:1, 5, 11), not by works (i.e., circumcision) or in keeping with the law. God's grace declares us (justified: not guilty) by what Jesus did for us by giving up His life for our sin debt and redeemed us and bought back our freedom. (Romans 3:24) When we were dead in our sins, Christ made us alive, and we are saved by grace. Paul told the Corinthians he depended on God's grace, not his own earthly wisdom .(2 Corinthians 1:12) The grace of God has been revealed and brings salvation to all people. (Titus 2:11) Paul prays for the grace of our Lord Jesus Christ to be with the believers in Rome. (Romans 16:20) Believers are to approach God with boldness (not in a prideful way) but with full assurance that He will give them mercy and grace in their time of need. (Hebrews 4:16)

GOD'S GRACE IS AMAZING!!!

We are cut off from grace when we try to make ourselves right with God by keeping the law. (Galatians 5:4) God has saved us and called us not by our works, but by His grace which was given to us by Christ Jesus before the world began. (2 Timothy 1:9) Look after each other so none of us will miss God's grace. (Hebrews 12:15) Grace allows us to serve God with reverence and godly fear. (Hebrews 12:28) Believers are to grow in grace by getting to know Christ more and more and be able to discern false teaching. (2 Peter 3:18) Beware of false teachers who believe that because of God's grace, we can live as we please. (Jude 4) We should never take God's grace for granted. (Romans 6:1-23) The Word (Jesus) was made flesh and dwelt among us full of grace and truth. (John 1:14, 17) The law was given to Moses by God, but grace and truth was given by Jesus Christ. (John 1:17)

GOD'S GRACE IS AMAZING!!!

Paul exhorts the Roman Christians for grace. (Romans 1:7) The law was given to show our sinfulness and as we sin more, grace abounds even more, (but not for us to sin more). (Romans 5:20) A faithful few have been chosen by God's grace and not by their works. (Romans 11:5-6) God's grace is sufficient for us and is all we need when we are weak and recognize that His power works best in our weakness. (2 Corinthians 12:9) Grace provided redemption through the blood of Jesus Christ which forgave our sins. He has showered us with kindness, wisdom, and prudence (insight). (Ephesians 1:7-8) Grace allows us to use our words to build people up and not tear them down. (Ephesians 4:29) Paul imparts grace to all believers who love Christ sincerely. (Ephesians 6:24) Husbands and wives are heirs of grace as the husband treats her with honor and understanding so his prayers will not be hindered. (1 Peter 3:7)

GOD'S GRACE IS AMAZING!!!

God resists the proud but gives grace to the humble. (1 Peter 5:5) God's grace has saved us from sin time and time again. (Nehemiah 9:28-31) God's grace is for everyone. (Luke 17:16) No matter how long we've been saved, we are the same in God's eyes and He is gracious. (Matthew 20:15-16) The law led us until Christ came and we, through faith, are made right with God. We are no longer under the law, but under grace and saved by it. (Galatians 3:24-25) God's grace saves us from sin's judgment (Romans 2:1) and allows us to live eternally with Him. (Colossians 1:21-22) What you learn from your parents will give you a crown of grace and clothe you with honor. (Proverbs 1:9) People often complain about the rain, but when God sends the rain, it is an expression of His grace. (Joel 2:23) God poured out a spirit of grace and prayer on David's family and Jerusalem. (Zechariah 12:10)

GOD'S GRACE IS AMAZING!!!

Stephen was a man full of God's grace and power and performed amazing miracles and signs among the people. (Acts 6:8) God's grace helps us to remain faithful. (Acts 13:43)

Acts 13:43 KJV
(www.bible.art)

"Now when the congregation was broken up, many of the Jews and religious proselytes (those converted to Judaism) followed Paul and Barnabas: who, speaking to them, persuaded them to continue in the grace of God."

F^1 = FAMILY: God Blesses The Family

In today's society, some of the family structure is far from the way God intended. We now see women married to women and men married to men. We see women raising their children alone as well as men because the parents are single, separated, or divorced. We also see women seeking sperm donations because they want a baby without the relationship of a man, and we see men seeking to adopt children because they are life partners or married to a man who cannot produce a baby in their union. We also have what we call blended families which include two families with children and the couple gets married, or a man or woman who already has children and marries someone without children and those future children are blended with the children that already exist. The family dynamics can go on and on but let us take a look at how God intended the family to be and how HE blesses the family with GRACE!

F^1 = FAMILY: God Blesses The Family

Then God said, "Let us make human beings in our image, to be like us. They will reign over the fish in the sea, the birds in the sky, the livestock, all the wild animals on the earth, and the small animals that scurry along the ground." So, God created human beings in His own image. In the image of God, He created them; male and female He created them. Then God blessed them and said, "Be fruitful and multiply. Fill the earth and govern it. Reign over the fish in the sea, the birds in the sky, and all the animals that scurry along the ground." (Genesis 1:26-28)

When God said, "to be like us," commentators and the Holy Spirit indicate He is speaking about the Trinity (i.e., Father, Son, and the Holy Spirit). As it is revealed in these verses, God intended for the original family to consist of male and female. When a man finds a wife, he finds a good thing and obtains favor with the Lord. (Proverbs 18:22)

F^1 = FAMILY: God Blesses The Family
God blesses the family with PARTNERSHIP: God Creates Eve for Adam

MARRIAGE IS GOD'S IDEA: (Genesis 2:18-24)

"Then the Lord God said, "It is not good for the man to be alone. I will make a helper who is exactly right for him." (Genesis 2:18) "So, the Lord God caused the man to fall into a deep sleep. While the man slept, the Lord God took out one of the man's ribs and closed up the opening. Then the Lord God made a woman from the rib and brought her to the man." "At last!" the man exclaimed. "This one is bone from my bone, and flesh from my flesh! She will be called 'woman' because she was taken from 'man.' This explains why a man leaves his father and mother and is joined to his wife, and the two are united into one. (Genesis 2:21-24)

The woman was made for man, not the other way around. (1 Corinthians 11:9)

F¹ = FAMILY: God Blesses The Family
How Can the Wife be a Blessing to her Husband?

As I think of my role as a married woman, there are many ways a wife can be a blessing to her husband. The Word refers to Eve as a "helpmeet," which means suitable help. (Genesis 2:18) There are many ways a wife can be "suitable help" for her husband. As I reflect upon the thirty-six (36) years of my marriage (2024), there are innumerable ways to be suitable help. The Hebrew translation of "helpmeet" is to aid or to help. One of the best ways I can help my husband is to submit to him as unto the Lord. (Ephesians 5:22, 24) (1 Peter 3:1)

What exactly does this mean? It means to willingly follow his leadership in Christ. You may say, what if my husband does not have a relationship with Christ? Well, the Word tells us that the Christian wife brings holiness to her marriage. (1 Corinthians 7: 14-16)

What exactly does that mean?

F^1 = FAMILY: God Blesses The Family
How Can the Wife be a Blessing to her Husband?

The Christian wife lives in a way that may persuade the unbelieving husband to become a Christian and the wife must continue to be a *positive influence*. I believe another way to be a blessing to your husband is to *pray for him*. Many times, we observe our husband's behavior, and we begin to criticize or to get angry at what we observe. Let's look at some examples: You enter the house, and you notice your husband's shoes in the middle of the floor. You can move the shoes then pray the Lord will help him remember "there is a place for everything" as my husband used to say when we moved into our new home in 2004. You notice your husband's area is untidy and he has left the house. You can tidy up the area and perhaps he will notice when he gets back home and if he does not, you can pray the Lord reminds him to do it the next time.

F^1 = FAMILY: God Blesses The Family
How Can the Wife be a Blessing to her Husband?

You may also ask him nicely to tidy up his area before leaving the house. It may happen and it may not, but at times, it may become a compromise.

Another way to help your husband is to help him with his many tasks. In this busy life, we all need a little help whether you work full time or stay at home full time.

*I remember when I left the workforce and stayed at home with my children for two (2) years, I used to get on the riding lawn mower and **mow the lawn** while the children stood at the door and watched. I believe it really blessed my husband to come home from work to see the lawn had been mowed. Even though I had multiple chores to do myself, as well as take care of my two (2) children, I made time to help him as well.*

F^1 = FAMILY: God Blesses The Family
How Can the Wife be a Blessing to her Husband?

I also remember when my children were a little older, my husband and I put up a wood privacy fence at our old home because we had an alley in the back of our house and many times people would just walk across the back yard and throw many cans and bottles in the yard ignoring the fact that we had a fur baby named "Snuggles" who lived out back. He also taught me how to hammer the boards and to use the air gun to attach the fence boards to the railings. He must have enjoyed my help because he accepted my request to assist him to make another privacy fence for one of his lawncare clients because her dogs continued to escape from her yard. If you have a hard-working husband like mine, you will have many opportunities to help him along with reminding him to come inside to eat lunch and dinner. My husband will work through lunch and dinner.

F^1 = FAMILY: God Blesses The Family
How Can the Wife be a Blessing to her Husband?

As his wife, I try to make life easier for him just as he does for me. He eats salad almost every day for lunch, so I try to prepare a couple of salads for him to eat whenever he takes a break from working throughout the week. We are both retired now so our schedules allow us to cater to each other more than when we both worked outside the home, but we did a pretty good job even when we were working outside the home! I remember my mother-in-love told me when I first married my husband to never start something you couldn't finish. She observed me preparing a plate of food for him and that is what she said, and I will always remember that and adhere to it. I do our laundry weekly and clean the house mostly when needed. I shop for groceries and pay bills online. We try our best to be considerate of each other's needs.

F¹ = FAMILY: God Blesses The Family
How Can the Wife be a Blessing to her Husband?

I. More Ways to Bless Your Husband from the Bible

a. Be trustworthy, enrich his life, bring him good and not harm, work with your hands, cook for him, be resourceful and manage the home well but most of all fear the LORD (Proverbs 31:10-31)!

b. Be willing to be taught how to live in a way that pleases God by not slandering or being a heavy drinker, be willing to teach younger women how to love their husbands and children and to live wisely, be pure, work at home and be submissive to your husband. (Titus 2:3-5)

c. Be a prudent (wise and intelligent) wife because she comes from the Lord. (Proverbs 19:14)

 Additional Bible Verses

{(1 Timothy 3:11), (Colossians 3:18), (1 Timothy 4:7)
(1 Corinthians 14:35), (Ephesians 5:22, 24), (1 Peter 3:1, 5)}

F^1 = FAMILY: God Blesses The Family
How Can the Wife be a Blessing to her Husband?

I. More Ways to Bless Your Husband from the Bible

    d. Be a crown to your husband. (Proverbs 12:4)

    e. Respect your husband. (Ephesians 5:33)

    f. Be quick to hear, slow to speak and slow to get angry. (James 1:19) (Ephesians 4:26)

    g. Forgive him. (Matthew 6:14-15).

    h. Show interest in what he is doing not just what you are doing. (Philippians 2:4)

    i. Speak life into him. (Proverbs 18:21)

    j. Satisfy his intimate needs. (1 Corinthians 7:3-5)

    k. Encourage him. (Romans 12:8a)

    l. Love him unconditionally. (1 Corinthians 13:4-7)

    m. Never stop praying. (1 Thessalonians 5:17)

F^1 = FAMILY: God Blesses The Family
How Can the Wife be a Blessing to her Husband?

I. More Ways to Bless Your Husband from the Bible

    n. Allow God to be the 3rd cord to keep you braided together. (Ecclesiastes 4:12)

    o. Allow God's word to instruct you in your marriage. (1 Corinthians 7:1-16)

    p. Remain faithful in your marriage. (Hebrews 13:4)

1. In your role as a wife, how have you been a blessing to your husband?

_____
_____

2. What could you do to improve what you're already doing?

_____
_____

F^1 = FAMILY: God Blesses The Family
How Can the Wife be a Blessing to her Husband?

From a Husband's Perspective

- *Allow your husband to be "manly."*
  (i.e., bowling, sports, man toys, movies, hunting, fishing, biking, etc.)

- *Tell him how important he is to the family.*

- *Rub his feet and massage his back.*

- *Cook dinner for him and prepare his plate.*

- *Be willing to dress up and go out on dates.*

- *Hold hands and hug him often.*

- *Always kiss him good morning and goodnight.*

- *Give him space to rest and refresh.*

- *Pray for him every day and throughout the day.*

- *Tell him you love him and mean it.*

- *Keep the kids and house quiet while he is resting.*

- *Listen attentively when he talks to you.*

- *Talk to him about everything.*

- *Don't move his "things" without telling him where they are.*

- *Be willing to compromise when you disagree.*

F^1 = FAMILY: God Blesses The Family
How Can the Husband be a Blessing to his Wife?

The husband has been called to be the *spiritual leader* in the home and is the head of the wife.

References: (1 Corinthians 11:3), (Ephesians 5:23), (1 Peter 3:7).

My husband and I have been married for thirty-six (36) years (2024) and I can honestly say he has been a blessing in my life. I could probably write a book about all the many wonderful ways he has been a blessing to me! After being married about three (3) years (1991), we had one daughter and a son on the way. I had been working out of town and commuting since 1985. The Lord began to prompt me to quit my job and stay at home. After about three (3) weeks of crying and praying, my husband agreed to the big shift in our income. Not only was that a leap of faith on my behalf, but it certainly was also on his behalf. He continued to work and provide for his family and household without any complaints. We made the necessary adjustments!

F^1 = FAMILY: God Blesses The Family
How Can the Husband be a Blessing to his Wife?

When God created Adam, He placed him in the Garden of Eden to care for it. This meant that he was supposed to work and take care of it. (Genesis 2:15) He was to be the manager over what God created (plants, animals, etc.) and maintained.

For us today, this means the husband is to **take care of the needs of his household because failure to do so makes him like an unbeliever.** (1 Timothy 5:8)

I remember how I admired and was impressed with my husband's ability to use his three (3) middle fingers to operate the calculator (without looking at the keys) as he was **balancing the checkbook.** Sure, I could do that while typing, but I had not mastered it with the calculator.

F^1 = FAMILY: God Blesses The Family
How Can the Husband be a Blessing to his Wife?

*My husband has many roles as a **financial manager**, **travel agent** (he plans and books most of our trips), **technician** (troubleshoots and repairs technology), **electrician** (installed electrical outlets, shop wiring, ceiling fans, etc.), **plumber** (installed sinks, toilets, showers and bathtubs), **landscaper** (maintains the lawn, plants, trees, etc.), **flooring installer, painter, window installer, grill master** (cooks the best ribs I have ever tasted), **mechanic** (repairs all our vehicles including the lawnmower and tractor), **carpenter** (built prayer boxes, VHS cabinet, privacy fences, cedar chests, decks, coat, and hat racks, etc.) **takes out the trash weekly, washes the dishes he uses**, wipes the sprinkles when he tinkles, tidies up his area, shops for household essentials (i.e., toilet paper, paper towels, plug ins, our favorite snacks, laundry aids, etc.).*

F^1 = FAMILY: God Blesses The Family
How Can the Husband be a Blessing to his Wife?

He washes a load of his clothes and towels occasionally and will help me to keep the laundry going by removing the clothes from the washer to the dryer after I have gone to bed. My husband has been very considerate and attentive to my needs throughout our marriage.

He cared for our children when I needed a nap and taught them how to be productive young adults by sharing his wisdom and experiences. He has been a listening ear for times when I needed a godly, objective opinion about life issues and problems.

He gives the best hugs and kisses me every day and night. He compliments me as I use my gifts to glorify God. He validates my appearance even when I may not do so, {(True beauty is from within-(1 Peter 3:3-4)} and we try to have weekly date nights.

F^1 = FAMILY: God Blesses The Family
How Can the Husband be a Blessing to his Wife?

From a Wife's Perspective

- Open the door for your wife.
- Run her bath water.
- Rub her feet and massage her back.
- Satisfy her intimate needs.
- Cook dinner for her.
- Take her out on dates weekly or monthly.
- Hold hands and hug her often.
- Always kiss her good morning and goodnight.
- Give her space to rest and refresh.
- Pray for her every day and throughout the day.
- Tell her you love her and mean it.
- Help her with the kids and chores whenever possible.
- Listen attentively when she talks to you.
- Talk to her about everything.
- Be willing to compromise when you disagree.

Supportive Bible Verses
{(Ephesians 5:25), (Colossians 3:19), (James 1:19), (Ephesians 4:26), (Matthew 6:14-15), (Philippians 2:4), (Proverbs 18:21), (Romans 12:8a), (1 Corinthians 7:1-16), (1 Corinthians 13:4-7), (1 Thessalonians 5:17), (Ecclesiastes 4:12), (1 Timothy 3:12), (1 Peter 3:7), (Hebrews 13:4)}

F^1 = FAMILY: God Blesses The Family
How Can the Father be a Blessing to the Family?

Our PERFECT example of a Father who is a blessing to the family would most definitely be our HEAVENLY FATHER!

More than two thousand years ago, He looked down on a dark and hopeless world filled with a group of people called humans and decided to send His sinless, only, begotten Son named Jesus in the form of a baby boy, born of a woman, at just the right time (Galatians 4:4-7) Jesus was sent by God to be the Savior of the world.
(1 John 4:9, 14) How many fathers do you know who will give up their only son? There are a few who may want to do so to avoid the responsibility of caring for them, but I believe most would not.

As God the Father, our Heavenly Father, is well acquainted with us, because He created us in His own image and likeness. (Genesis 1:27) Without a doubt, He knows how to be a blessing to the family.

F^1 = FAMILY: God Blesses The Family
How Can the Father be a Blessing to the Family?

We are told in the Bible that families of every nation would be blessed as a result of having the faith of Abraham's descendants (Genesis 12:1-3) That is why the Bible refers to Abraham as the "father" of many nations. (Genesis 17:4-5) Our Heavenly Father is a blessing to families by:

- ✝ *Offering us everlasting life (John 3:16)*
- ✝ *Lavishing His love on His children (1 John 3:1)*
- ✝ *Giving us the privilege to see His kingdom (John 3:3)*
- ✝ *Sealing us with the Holy Spirit (Ephesians 1:13)*
- ✝ *Offering us forgiveness (1 John 1:9)*
- ✝ *Giving us spiritual blessings (Ephesians 1:3)*
- ✝ *Supplying all of our needs (Philippians 4:19)*
- ✝ *Protecting us from danger (Psalm 18:30)*
- ✝ *Being our all in all (1 Corinthians 15:28)*

F^1 = FAMILY: God Blesses The Family
How Can the Father be a Blessing to the Family?

Now that we have examined how our Heavenly Father blesses the family, let us take a look at our earthly father. In our society, many children grow up without a father in the household because of single parenthood, divorce, and the death of a parent. As I reminisce about my childhood, I don't remember much about the presence of a father in my home. I remember a couple encounters with him as a pre-teen and a teenager after he and my mother divorced when I was about four (4) years old. A father can be a blessing to the family by following the leadership of his Heavenly Father. (1 Corinthians 11:3) Once this takes place, the father in the home can be a blessing in many ways. The Bible tells us that a father is to nurture and raise up a child in the admonition of the Lord. (Ephesians 6:4) This means the father is to educate, train, discipline, and sometimes rebuke and strongly warn the child. How is this a blessing you may ask? A child who is disciplined is blessed. (Psalm 94:12)

F^1 = FAMILY: God Blesses The Family
How Can the Father be a Blessing to the Family?

A child who listens to his father's instructions is wise. (Proverbs 13:1) The Bible records that God disciplines those whom He loves. Besides, we endured the discipline of our earthly fathers, should we not endure the discipline of our Heavenly Father much more (Hebrews 12:9)?

Discipline is more painful than pleasant for the moment, but it produces the peaceful fruit of righteousness to those who have been trained by it. (Hebrews 12:11)
A father in the home can be a blessing to his wife.
(See the previous section about a husband being a blessing to his wife).

He can also be a blessing to his children. As we raised our children, my husband was the gentle, humble disciplinarian. He was quick to talk to the children and I was quick to spank and talk at the same time!

F¹ = FAMILY: God Blesses The Family
How Can the Father be a Blessing to the Family?

I think that since most women are emotional creatures, we tend to be driven by our emotions (i.e., anger, sadness, disappointment, etc.). My children would prefer their father to spank them rather than myself because they said I would "preach" and spank at the same time and it took longer. I thought that was hilarious. Parents are encouraged to discipline their children as it will bring peace of mind and gladness of heart. (Proverbs 29:17) They are instructed to train them up in the way they should go and when they are old, they will not depart from it. (Proverbs 22:6) If children are corrected with the rod, they will not die but the correction will deliver their soul from hell. (Proverbs 23:13-14) Fathers are encouraged not to provoke their children to anger by the way they treat them but to bring them up in the nurture and admonition of the Lord. (Ephesians 6:4)

F¹ = FAMILY: God Blesses The Family
How Can the Father be a Blessing to the Family?

The Bible reminds us in (Proverbs 13:24) that if we spare the rod of discipline, we hate the child, but those who love their children care enough to discipline them. The father can bless his children in various ways such as: teach his son about becoming a man, how to drive, how to mow the lawn, change the oil in a car, use power tools, apply himself in sports and education, how to do household maintenance, how to manage his household finances, how to be a son, friend, brother, husband, etc. The father can also bless his children by **praying for them** and **being an example** to his daughter of how a man should treat her during the dating years and possibly marriage thereafter. He can teach her how to drive, change a tire, use a power tool, mow the lawn and how to manage her finances and how to treat her husband. The possibilities are endless. The most important lesson a son (or daughter) can learn from a father is how to be a child of God. (Galatians 3:26)

F^1 = FAMILY: God Blesses The Family
How Can the Father be a Blessing to his Family?

Reflection Activity

1. In your role as a father, how have you been a blessing to your family? (In relation to your wife and children)

_____
_____
_____
_____

2. What are some things you can do to improve in your role as a father?

_____
_____
_____
_____

3. What do you need God to help you do?

_____
_____
_____

F¹ = FAMILY: God Blesses The Family
How is the Family Blessed with a Mother?

There are two (2) mothers that come to mind when I think about the Bible, and they are: Mary (the mother of Jesus and Hannah the mother of Samuel). Let us take a look at the life of Mary leading up to her becoming the mother of Jesus. Mary was a young teenager engaged to be married to Joseph. Before the marriage, the angel Gabriel visited Mary to give her a message that she would become the mother of the Son of God (Jesus Christ). (Luke 1:26-38)

With Mary being a virgin, she didn't understand how this could happen, but she accepted what God wanted and told the angel Gabriel that she received his message and that she wanted everything he said to come true.

In this day and age, could you imagine being a teenage virgin, engaged and impregnated by the Holy Spirit?

Do you know how difficult that message would be for the people of this world to receive and believe? Mary was willing to risk being ostracized, rejected and unmarried. She graciously accepted and submitted to God's will as His humble, obedient servant.

F^1 = FAMILY: God Blesses The Family
How is the Family Blessed with a Mother?

Mary believed the Lord would do what He said, and she began to praise Him before it came to pass. (Luke 1:45-56) So, this young mother-to-be was blessed, because she had **faith in God**, was chosen by Him and was not ashamed to confess her faith in Him. Our faith in God and His word, gives us the wisdom to be a blessing to our families. After the angel visited her fiancé Joseph, he was convinced that Mary had conceived by the power of the Holy Spirit, and he followed the angel's directions for him to marry her, but she remained a virgin until after the birth of Jesus. (Matthew 1:18-25) Mary was a blessing to her family as she and her husband Joseph were **obedient** to the Law of Moses when they presented Him to the Lord and **dedicated** Him back to the Lord when He was eight (8) days old. (Luke 2:21-24) After Jesus became a young lad at age twelve (12), Mary also accepted that her Son was called to do God's will even when she and her husband didn't always understand. (Luke 2:41-51)

F^1 = FAMILY: God Blesses The Family
How is the Family Blessed with a Mother?

Mary's actions at the wedding in Cana was evidence that she had faith in what God would do through her Son even when she didn't know how He was going to do it. (John 2:1-12) Mary was supportive of her grown Son's ministry as she met continually with Him and His disciples for prayer (Acts 1:14) and she was also present with Him during His crucifixion. (John 19:25)

So, let's recap how the mother of Jesus (Mary) was a blessing to her family:

- ❖ Faith and trust in God
- ❖ Sensitive to the message of God
- ❖ Obedience to God
- ❖ Praised the Lord for His faithfulness
- ❖ Followed the sanctity of marriage
- ❖ Accepted God's will for her Son
- ❖ Supported her Son's Ministry

F^1 = FAMILY: God Blesses The Family
How is the Family Blessed with a Mother?

Now that we have discussed the most famous mother of the Bible, (Mary the mother of Jesus), let's take a look at the life of Hannah and how she was a blessing to her family. As I read (1st Samuel 1-2), I envisioned a woman of faith who was obedient to her God and her husband. Hannah's husband, Elkanah, had two wives, herself and Peninnah. Hannah didn't have any children, but Peninnah did. Peninnah made fun of Hannah because she was considered barren and couldn't have children. Hannah and her family were worshippers of the true living God. She and her family were committed to traveling to Shiloh each year to worship and sacrifice to the Lord God Almighty at the Tabernacle. There was a time in particular when Hannah and her family had traveled to Shiloh to worship the Lord at the Tabernacle and Hannah went in during supper to pray to the Lord. As Hannah prayed, she was in deep anguish and cried sorrowfully to the Lord.

F¹ = FAMILY: God Blesses The Family
How is the Family Blessed with a Mother?

She promised the Lord that if He would look down on her sorrow and answer her prayer for a son, then she would give her son back to the Lord. She told the Lord the child would belong to Him his entire life and his hair would never be cut signifying his dedication to the Lord. As she was praying, Eli the priest of the Tabernacle, noticed that her mouth was moving but no sound came out. He thought she had been drinking and asked her why she came to the Tabernacle drunk and he demanded she throw away her wine. Hannah then told Eli she wasn't drunk but she was very sad and was pouring her heart out to God. She asked Eli not to consider her to be a wicked woman because she was praying out of anguish and sorrow. Eli then said if that was the case, "cheer-up" and may the God of Israel give to her what she asked for. Hannah thanked Eli and went back to her supper because she was no longer sad.

F¹ = FAMILY: God Blesses The Family
How is the Family Blessed with a Mother?

The next morning the whole family got up early to go to worship the Lord once more. They then returned home to Ramah and when Elkanah slept with Hannah, the Lord remembered her prayer request and she conceived a son and when the time had come, she gave birth to a son. She named him Samuel who in the Hebrew means: "asked of God" or "heard of God," because she asked the Lord for him. The next year, the family went to Shiloh as usual, but Hannah did not go because she wanted to wait until the baby Samuel was weaned and at which time, she would leave him there permanently. Her husband agreed that if she thought it was best and told her to stay for that period of time and that the Lord would help her keep her promise. I would think that Elkanah probably felt as if Hannah was having a difficult time letting go of her son Samuel and that she used nursing as an excuse to have more time with him. Keep in mind that the customary age for weaning was three (3) years old.

F^1 = FAMILY: God Blesses The Family
How is the Family Blessed with a Mother?

How many of us mothers would be willing to spend three (3) years nursing and loving a child only to give him up to the Lord? When we have "dedication" services for our babies, we are only making a ceremonial vow. We don't physically give up our babies as Hannah did. We only make a vow to raise our children in the admonition of the Lord. (Ephesians 6:4) When Samuel was weaned, Hannah took him to the Tabernacle along with a three (3) year old bull for sacrifice and half a bushel of flour and some wine. After sacrificing the bull, they took Samuel to Eli the priest. Hannah asked Eli if he remembered her. She told him that she was the woman who stood there several years prior petitioning the Lord to give her that same child and He honored her request. She explained that she was now giving her son Samuel back to the Lord and that he would belong to the Lord his whole life and they worshipped the Lord there in the Tabernacle.

F¹ = FAMILY: God Blesses The Family
How is the Family Blessed with a Mother?

In (1 Samuel 2:1-10), Hannah gives God a prayer of praise. In verse 1, Hannah's heart was rejoicing in the Lord because of the blessings He bestowed upon her. Hannah now had an answer to her enemy's (Peninnah) taunting, as she was delighting in God's deliverance; even though Hannah didn't respond when Peninnah was teasing and taunting her because everyone thought she was barren. When our enemies tease and taunt us, we don't have to respond with angry words of retaliation. God will silence our enemies in due season. In verse 2, Hannah continued to reverence God by acknowledging His Holiness, Uniqueness, Strength, Firmness, and Consistent Character. In verse 3, Hannah began to warn Peninnah of her proud, haughty, and arrogant behavior (Proverbs 16:18) reminds us that pride goes before destruction and a haughty spirit before a fall. She informed her that God knew all of her deeds and He would judge her for all she had done.

F^1 = FAMILY: God Blesses The Family
How is the Family Blessed with a Mother?

In verse 4, Hannah wanted everyone who was operating in their "own power", to be reminded that God in all His omnipotence (all powerful) could cause the "so-called" "mighty" to be mighty no more (Be strong in the Lord and in the power of His might: Ephesians 6:10) and to remind the weak that they could now be strong (2 Corinthians 12:9b...His strength is made perfect in weakness). In verse 5, Hannah tells us that those that are full would now be starving and those who were starving would now be full. The barren woman now has seven children and the woman with many children would have no more. In verse 6, Hannah wanted to praise God even more by acknowledging that God gives life and death by bringing some down to the grave and raising others up. In verse 7, Hannah continued in her praises to God by stating that He makes one rich and another poor and that He lifts one up and brings another down.

F¹ = FAMILY: God Blesses The Family
How is the Family Blessed with a Mother?

In verse 8, God lifts the poor from the dust and a pile of ashes and treats them like princes and exalts them by placing them in seats of honor (1 Peter 5:6 Humble yourselves therefore under the mighty hand of God, that He may exalt you in due time) Hannah continues to acknowledge God's sovereignty by proclaiming that the earth is the Lord's and He has set order in the world.

(1 Corinthians 10:26) The earth is the Lord's and the fullness thereof). In verse 9, Hannah praised God even further by stating that God will protect His godly ones and the wicked would perish in darkness and no one would succeed by their own strength.

(Psalm 91:11-12 For He shall give his angels charge over thee, to keep thee in all thy ways. They shall bear thee up in their hands, lest thou dash thy foot against a stone.) In verse 10, Hannah reminds us that those who fight against the Lord will be broken.

F¹ = FAMILY: God Blesses The Family
How is the Family Blessed with a Mother?

In (Matthew 21:42-44), Jesus is the stone that the builders rejected but He is the cornerstone that will either be built upon, or be tripped over and during judgment, many will be crushed by Him. He punishes them with thunder from heaven and His judgment is apparent throughout the Earth. He empowers his kings with strength and increases His anointed ones' might.

In (1 Samuel 2:19-21), Hannah continued to see Samuel each year when she came to the Tabernacle for Worship and to bring him a coat that she made for him that was very much like Eli's coat.

Each year the priest Eli would bless Elkanah and Hannah by asking the Lord to give them more children to replace the child (Samuel) that she gave back to the Lord. Hannah indeed was blessed even more with three (3) additional sons and two (2) daughters while Samuel continued to grow before the Lord.

F^1 = FAMILY: God Blesses The Family
How is the Family Blessed with a Mother?

Now, let us recap how Hannah (Samuel's mother) was a blessing to her family:

- *She and her family worshipped the true and living God*
- *She didn't allow her problems to keep her from worshipping God*
- *She did not retaliate when she was mistreated*
- *She prayed persistent and effective prayers to God*
- *She asked God for what she wanted even though her situation seemed hopeless*
- *She was willing to miss a meal to seek God*
- *She made a promise to God and kept it*
- *God rewarded her when He answered her prayers*

Hannah was a good example of a godly wife, mother and servant of God who was rewarded for her faithfulness to God!

F^1 = FAMILY: God Blesses The Family
How is the Family Blessed with a Mother?

My mother has been in my life for over sixty-one (61) years (2024), and she has truly been a blessing in my life. I can commence by stating that she blessed me by allowing the seed of my life to be planted in her womb even though I was born about two months early.

The Lord knew this would happen and he took care of me through the doctors and nurses assigned to my care. As adults and children of God, we sometimes ask "why?" I began to ask God "why?" when things were not going my way and I wanted a way out or so I thought.

I asked God why He allowed me to live when I was born two (2) months early. As a child, I grew up with three (3) brothers. I lived a pretty sheltered life because I was the only girl up until age eleven (11) and the middle child after the birth of my sister. I can't recall a multitude of events from my early childhood, but I recall a few events quite vividly. As a woman in her (then) 50's, I used to look back on my childhood to appreciate where I came from and who I have become.

F^1 = FAMILY: God Blesses The Family
How is the Family Blessed with a Mother?

I used to wonder as a ten-year-old girl, why I had to do laundry. I remember in 1973 that we had a washer and not a dryer. We had to hang clothes out on the line in our back yard. I was too short to reach the clothesline, so I had to take a chair outside to stand up on and as I hung the clothes, I slid the basket while avoiding the sticker briars and fire ants. I also remember having to clean the house regularly and cook at the age of 13.

My mom was and still is a good cook at her present age. She taught me how to cook everything she knew how to cook. It wasn't very easy. I remember the first batch of biscuits and the first batch of fried chicken. The biscuits weren't the best and the chicken was not all done. Before I became a better cook, my brothers used to tease me that it wasn't as good as Mom's, but it would do. Why did this happen? I believe the Lord was allowing my Mom to train me to be the ideal woman.

See (Proverbs 22:6; Proverbs 31).

F^1 = FAMILY: God Blesses The Family
How is the Family Blessed with a Mother?

There have been times when I recalled having to take care of my duties as a wife and mother and it caused a smile to appear upon my face because it was a reminder that if my mother had not taught me how to become a woman, I would just be going with the flow of life trying to figure things out. My mother was a blessing to me as a daughter by doing the following:

- Teaching me how to take care of my body
- Teaching me how to take care of my sister
- Teaching me how to do laundry
- Teaching me how to cook, clean, iron, and sew
- Teaching me how to manage money and pay bills
- Teaching me how to be organized
- Teaching me how to drive
- Encouraging me to learn to type in high school
- Encouraging me to get married before having children
- Giving motherly love, advice, and discipline when needed
- Assisting me financially as a student/young adult
- Helping me with my children as needed
- Inspiring me with her longevity and perseverance

F^1 = FAMILY: God Blesses The Family
How is the Family Blessed with a Mother?

On the previous page, I discussed how a mother is a blessing from a daughter's point of view.

In this section, I will discuss how a mother can be a blessing from a son's point of view. My husband has stated that his mother was a blessing to his family by:

- Taking care of him
- Providing discipline when needed
- Nurturing him
- Sharing her faith
- Praying for her children
- Sharing the food from her garden
- Always having food on the table
- Always shared a smile and an embrace

F¹ = FAMILY: God Blesses The Family
How is the Family Blessed with a Mother?

Reflection Activity

1. In your role as a mother, how have you been a blessing to your family? (In relation to your husband and children)

_____
_____
_____
_____
_____

2. What are some things you can do to improve in your role as a mother?

_____
_____
_____
_____

3. What do you need God to help you do?

_____
_____
_____

F^1 = FAMILY: God Blesses The Family
How is the Family Blessed with a Son?

Let's observe the Biblical role of a son.

According to the New Living Translation definition, a son is defined as a parent's male child or descendant further removed; spiritual heir (of Christ) (Romans 8:16-17) and the relationship of Jesus to the heavenly Father.

The most important son I learned about was the Son of God (Jesus Christ).

As a twelve (12) year old girl, I was introduced to Him and wanted to have a relationship with Him.

In (Isaiah 9:6) the prophecy is told that Jesus Christ would be born unto us and given to us, and He would bear the weight of the government on His shoulders and His name would be called Wonderful Counselor, the Mighty God, the Everlasting Father, the Prince of Peace. In (Matthew 1:21), we are told that Mary would bring forth a Son and His name would be called Jesus who would save people from their sins. God was well pleased with His Son. (Matthew 3:17)

F^1 = FAMILY: God Blesses The Family
How is the Family Blessed with a Son?

Jesus, the Son of God, knew that He could do nothing of Himself but only what He saw the Father do and He did likewise. (John 5:19) Is this not so profound in our culture? The son often imitates or emulates the father. Therefore, the earthly father needs to imitate/emulate God, our Heavenly Father. God loved the world so much that He gave His one and only Son to save us so that we would not perish and have everlasting life. (John 3:16) Anyone who denies the Son, does not have the Father either, but anyone who acknowledges the Son, has the Father also. (1 John 2:23) In other words, you cannot say you believe in the God the Father and not believe in God the Son Jesus Christ. When the Son of Man returns, it will be like in Noah's day when people were celebrating and not realizing that the flood was coming and swept them all away. (Matthew 24:37-39)

F¹ = FAMILY: God Blesses The Family
How is the Family Blessed with a Son?

How is the Son of God (Jesus) a blessing to families?

- ✝ He was sent by His Father to save us
- ✝ He respected His parents
- ✝ He was obedient unto God even unto death
- ✝ He loves everyone unconditionally
- ✝ He was kind and forgiving to His enemies
- ✝ He prayed for His family, friends, and enemies
- ✝ He desired the will of God more than His own
- ✝ He endured a shameful death to give us life

📚 Supportive Bible Verses

{(John 3:16), (Luke 2:51), (Philippians 2:8)}

{(1 Corinthians 13), (Luke 23:34), (John 19:26-27)}

{(Matthew 5:43-44), (Matthew 6:14-15)}

{(Luke 3:21-22), (Luke 22:42)}

F^1 = FAMILY: God Blesses The Family
How is the Family Blessed with a Son?

Now that I've introduced some of you (and reintroduced others) to the Son of God and how He is a blessing to all families, we can discuss how the earthly son can be a blessing to the family. I remember asking God for a son and he blessed me with a son when my daughter was seventeen (17) months old. In my human plan, I wanted my daughter to be potty trained before getting pregnant with my son because I didn't want two (2) babies in diapers. At the time my son was born, I was a stay-at-home Mom. We had to find ways to be conservative and one of the ways we executed this plan was to use cloth diapers instead of disposable diapers. My son was mild mannered and did not cry much and as a toddler, he found ways to engage himself by playing with his toys. He even enjoyed taking naps which was a welcomed trait. He grew up to be a fine young man who did well in school, was active in sports and had a small circle of friends and became industrious and successful in his Computer Science field.

F^1 = FAMILY: God Blesses The Family
How is the Family Blessed with a Son?

When I reflect upon the relationship my son had with my husband, I am reminded of the benefits and blessings a son can bring to a family. A son can bless his family by assisting with the household chores, helping with the care of younger siblings, being a playmate to his siblings, being a positive leader to his siblings, accepting the Biblical teaching of his parents and church leaders, etc. According to the Bible, children are a gift from God, and they are a reward from Him. (Psalm 127:3)

There are many sons who have had to take on the role as a father-figure in cases where the father passed away or was not present. They had to take on the duties of attaining a job, paying bills, assisting in managing the household and raising younger siblings. This has happened a lot in many cultures.

F¹ = FAMILY: God Blesses The Family
How is the Family Blessed with a Son?

A son can be a blessing to the family by listening to his father, not despising his mother in old age, seeking truth, getting wisdom, discipline, and good judgment. Godly children bring joy to their fathers, and it is a pleasure to have children who are wise. (Proverbs 23:22-24, 26)

A son is blessed when he gives his heart to the Lord and takes delight in following His ways. Even children are known by the way they act, whether their conduct is pure and right. (Proverbs 20:11) A wise son fears the Lord and the king and does not associate with rebels because he does not know what punishment will come from both the Lord and the king. (Proverbs 24:21-22)

A son can reap the benefits of a long life along with peace if he obeys the commandments of God. (Proverbs 3:1-2)

A wise son does not overextend himself by agreeing to help a friend in need but should act responsibly so that his family does not suffer. (Proverbs 6:1-4)

F^1 = FAMILY: God Blesses The Family
How is the Family Blessed with a Son?

These verses are not discouraging generosity but encouraging the use of wisdom and responsibility in your giving. In other words, don't agree to pay someone else's debts and not be able to pay your own. Speaking of paying debts, a wise son works all summer, but a lazy son sleeps away opportunities to be productive and brings about shame. (Proverbs 10:5)

A wise son must NOT love his parents more than he loves God. (Matthew 10:37) Children who are taught by the Lord will enjoy great peace. (Isaiah 54:13) During Biblical times, the firstborn son was a symbol of strength, dignity, and power. (Genesis 49:3)

He inherited the authority and responsibilities of the father and the right to a double portion of the family estate in the event the father died. The father had the right to give the birthright to a younger son as in the cases of Jacob, Esau, (Genesis 49:1-4) Manasseh and Ephraim (Genesis 48:13-19).

F¹ = FAMILY: God Blesses The Family
How is the Family Blessed with a Son?

A father in Biblical times (and even now) wanted to have a son so that he would have an heir to inherit his estate and to keep the family name alive.

Since Jesus Christ is the only and firstborn (Psalm 89:27) Son of God, He is the heir of God and that makes us believers co-heirs with Christ. (Romans 8:17)

How are WE blessed as a co-heir (male or female) of Jesus Christ? Everything God promised to Jesus Christ belongs to us. As believers in Jesus Christ, our inheritance includes salvation (Hebrews 1:14), eternal life (1 Peter 1:4), and shared authority with Jesus Christ (Revelation 3:21). So, whether you're an heir by biological birth, adoption, and/or rebirth through faith in Jesus, you are blessed!

Additional Bible Verses
{(John 3:3, 7), (1 Peter 1:3, 23), (Romans 8:14-16)}
{(Acts 4:12), (Ephesians 1:13-14), (2 Corinthians 5:17)}

F¹ = FAMILY: God Blesses The Family
How is the Family Blessed with a Son?

Reflection Activity

1. In your role as a son, how have you been a blessing to your family? (In relation to your mother, father, and siblings)

___
___
___
___
___

2. What are some things you can do to improve in your role as a son?

___
___
___
___
___

3. What do you need God to help you do?

___
___
___

F^1 = FAMILY: God Blesses The Family
How is the Family Blessed with a Daughter?

As I discussed in the previous section about how a mother is a blessing to her family, the daughter can also be a blessing to her family. The Bible makes several references to a daughter (daughter of Zion (Jerusalem), daughter of Judah, etc.). These references are used basically to depict God as a caring, patient, and loving Father to His people. We are informed in the Bible that children are a gift from God and are considered a reward from Him. (Psalm 127:3) No child should be considered a "mistake" no matter the circumstances (i.e., timing, failed birth-control, rape, incest, premarital sex, etc.) of their conception because ultimately, God is in control of life and death. (Deuteronomy 32:39a)

According to merriam-webster.com, a daughter is defined as: a female offspring especially of human parents, (b): a female adopted child, or (c): a human female descendant.

F^1 = FAMILY: God Blesses The Family
How is the Family Blessed with a Daughter?

The Bible also discusses a multitude of daughters and their roles with their families. My purpose in discussing a few will be to show how they were a blessing to their families. Moses's father-in-law Reuel (AKA: Jethro) had seven (7) daughters. He was the priest of Midian, and his name "Jethro" is a reference to his official title as "His excellency." One day as the daughters were drawing water for their father's flocks, they were unexpectantly protected by Moses as some shepherds drove them away. One of Reuel's daughters named Zipporah, was given to Moses as his wife. She was a blessing to her family by preventing God from killing her husband, Moses when she circumcised their son. The covenant God had with Abraham required that all his male descendants be circumcised. Not only was Zipporah a hard-working helpful daughter but she was also a supportive wife to Moses.

{(Genesis 17:9-11, 13-14), (Exodus 2:21), (Exodus 4:24-26), (Exodus 18:2)}

F¹ = FAMILY: God Blesses The Family
How is the Family Blessed with a Daughter?

The Bible also mentions another set of five daughters (Mahlah, Noah, Hoglah, Milcah, and Tirzah) whose father was named Zelophehad. These daughters were a blessing to their family and the nation of Israel by advocating for land for daughters who had a deceased father and no brothers to inherit family land and who also helped Moses to set a legal precedent for the rest of Israel to follow regarding men inheriting land rightfully owned by their wives prior to marriage (Numbers 27:1-11; 36:1-13) www.gotquestions.org. I remember in the first year and a half of our marriage, we began discussing having children. I wanted to have a daughter and a son. I wanted a child of each gender because I only wanted to experience pregnancy twice. My husband on the other hand stated that he wanted to be half (1/2) the man his father was by having seven (7) children compared to his Dad's fourteen (14). God did not allow that to happen.

F^1 = FAMILY: God Blesses The Family
How is the Family Blessed with a Daughter?

I can recall the day of my daughter's birth as if it were yesterday. After my daughter's birth in 1990, I was in the hospital room and when they brought her to see me, she was wrapped snuggly in a multi-colored blanket, and she was wearing a pink hood. When they placed her in my arms, she was moving her head from side to side as if she was looking for someone. I always believed she was looking for her Dad who had not come back into the room at that time. Our daughter was truly a delight to raise and to get to know. She was beautiful, bright, friendly, helpful, loving, and inquisitive. There was a time as she was discovering writing her letters, she wrote a letter on her Magna Doodle Toy and showed it to me, and I was so enthralled because I had never taught her to write but we had introduced identifying letters, numbers, colors, and shapes by the age of three (3).

F¹ = FAMILY: God Blesses The Family
How is the Family Blessed with a Daughter?

She was **helpful** with her brother as well. She would get diapers and sippy cups for his care. She was also an active **playmate** for him as well. She affectionately gave him **hugs and kisses** as well. She was also no stranger to most people, especially her family members, as she would often stay the night with them. She did well in school, was active in cheerleading, had a small circle of friends and grew up to be a young woman who is **kind, generous, compassionate, attentive, and intentional.** She likes to have fun, spend time with family, is a woman of faith and loves the Lord with deep devotion, she has become an exceptional wife, mother, counselor, and rising entrepreneur. A daughter can be a blessing to the family by listening to her father, not despising her mother in old age, seeking truth, getting wisdom, discipline, and good judgment. Godly children bring joy to their fathers, and it is a pleasure to have children who are wise. (Proverbs 23:22-24, 26) A daughter is blessed when she gives her heart to the Lord and takes delight in following His ways.

F^1 = FAMILY: God Blesses The Family
How is the Family Blessed with a Daughter?

Even children are known by the way they act, whether their conduct is pure and right. (Proverbs 20:11) A wise daughter fears the Lord and the king and does not associate with rebels because she does not know what punishment will come from both the Lord and the king. (Proverbs 24:21-22) A daughter can reap the benefits of a long life and peace if she obeys the commandments of God. (Proverbs 3:1-2) A wise daughter does not overextend herself by agreeing to help a friend in need but should act responsibly so that her family does not suffer. (Proverbs 6:1-4) These verses are not discouraging generosity but encouraging the use of wisdom and responsibility in your giving. In other words, don't agree to pay someone else's debts and not be able to pay your own. Speaking of paying debts, a wise daughter works all summer, but a lazy daughter sleeps away opportunities to be productive and brings about shame. (Proverbs 10:5)

F^1 = FAMILY: God Blesses The Family
How is the Family Blessed with a Daughter?

A wise daughter must NOT love her parents more than she loves God. (Matthew 10:37) Children who are taught by the Lord will enjoy great peace. (Isaiah 54:13)

Before concluding this section, I would be remiss if I didn't mention that the Lord blessed me with two "bonus" daughters (aka god daughters) one of which I met and taught while she was in the 6th grade back in 2002. She sends me texts to check on me and will call as well and she blessed me by adopting me as her "god mama" and she was helpful in my classroom by helping sort graded papers, labeling folders and filing my paperwork, helping to clean and organize my desks, assisting with my bulletin boards and anything else I needed help with.

My other bonus daughter blessed me as I taught her in 8th grade back in 1994. She assisted me with grading papers and she also used to babysit my toddler children and will text me almost every Mother's Day and other special holidays. We are all still in touch today even after so much time has passed!

Please note the word "son" has been changed to "daughter" in the previous verses above because I believe these verses are relevant to sons and daughters. It was NOT my intention to add to or take away from the original meaning or interpretation of God's word
(Deuteronomy 4:2)

F¹ = FAMILY: God Blesses The Family
How is the Family Blessed with a Daughter?

Reflection Activity

1. In your role as a daughter, how have you been a blessing to your family? (In relation to your parents and siblings)

_____
_____
_____
_____

2. What are some things you can do to improve in your role as a daughter?

_____
_____
_____
_____

3. What do you need God to help you do?

_____
_____
_____

F^1 = FAMILY: God Blesses The Family
How is the Family Blessed with a Brother?

I was raised and grew up with three (3) brothers. They were all unique in their own way. I was in the middle of five (5) children. I had two (2) brothers who were older and a brother who was younger. My oldest brother (God rest his soul) could be described as a "cool dude" who lived an adventurous life. My second oldest brother could be described as an industrious young man who was always seeking to improve himself. My youngest brother (God rest his soul) could be described as a carefree lover of nature.

They were a blessing in my life by spending time with me, teaching me how to be athletic, protecting me from bullies and womanizers, helping me with chores, teaching me how to drive, guiding my major choice in college, and showing love to me and my family.

I must also mention that I have a brother on my Dad's side who blesses me with his random texts, hugs, and dances at family events. For those who do not have a brother, Jesus is a friend that sticks closer than a brother and He will ALWAYS be a blessing in your life. (Proverbs 18:24b)

F^1 = FAMILY: God Blesses The Family
How is the Family Blessed with a Brother?

The previous page depicts how my brothers were a blessing to me, their sister. In this section, my husband has shared how his brothers were a blessing to him from a brother's perception. My husband had six (6) brothers. Brothers can be a blessing to the family by:

- Always being there for each other

- Sharing knowledge

- Sharing clothes

- Sharing transportation

- Sharing encouragement

- Teaming up in sports

- Assisting with the needs of siblings

F^1 = FAMILY: God Blesses The Family
How is the Family Blessed with a Brother?

Now that we have explored the blessings of having a brother in our personal relationships, let us consider the Biblical perspective of the blessings in other brotherly relationships. One of my favorite Bible verses is (Proverbs 17:17 KJV). It states that a friend loves at all times and a brother is born for adversity. For a long time, I focused on the a-part of that verse and not the b-part.

After researching the verse years ago, I discovered that it meant that the role of a brother is for him to be helpful during times of adversity. I can truly say while growing up, my brothers were impactful during some of my times of adversity.

The first brother in the Bible that comes to mind is Joseph. I could write an entire book on the life of Joseph; however, I will attempt to focus on how he was a blessing to his family.

F¹ = FAMILY: God Blesses The Family
How is the Family Blessed with a Brother?

Joseph was the son of Jacob and Rachel. He was one of twelve (12) sons and had one (1) sister. He was labeled as his father's "favorite." As a teenager, Joseph was immensely helpful to his family by tending to his father's flocks, checking up on his older brothers and providing food for them as they worked. He also shared the revelation of his dreams with his entire family which did not end so well for him or so it seemed. (Genesis 37:2-36) In spite of the adversities Joseph faced with his brothers, he was still favored by God and He continued to be with him and used him to bless his family and the people of Israel and Egypt. Joseph continued to be a blessing by honoring God while being tempted. (Genesis 39:7-9)

He also managed Pharoah's affairs as the second in command (Genesis 41:37-46), he offered food, land, forgiveness, and provisions to his family, even after they sold him as a slave. (Genesis 45:1-15; 47:5-12; 50:16-20)

F^1 = FAMILY: God Blesses The Family
How is the Family Blessed with a Brother?

Another brother from the Bible who comes to mind is David. His story and interaction with his father and brothers are somewhat similar to Joseph's. The number one attribute that comes to mind is that he was known to be a "**man after God's own heart.**" (Acts 13:22)
That is a blessing in itself. There are many words to describe David such as: shepherd, poet, musician, etc., however, these words only paint a positive view of David's life. The Bible also portrays David as an adulterer, liar, and a murderer. In this section, we will focus on the positive ways David was a blessing to his family. David was the son of Jesse and he had seven (7) brothers: Eliab, Abinadab, Abital, Maacah, Haggith, Eglah and Shammah. David was a blessing to his family by being **obedient to his father** while tending sheep and taking food to his older brothers and checking up on them as they worked for King Saul. David was also a blessing to his family and the people of Israel by his courageous plight to defeat the giant Goliath which resulted in the reward of a wife (Michal) for David and exemption from taxes for his father's family.
    Please read these verses: (1 Samuel 16 thru 18).

F¹ = FAMILY: God Blesses The Family
How is the Family Blessed with a Brother?

In light of David being a major character in the Bible, I would be remiss not to mention more ways he was a blessing to his family. David continued to be a blessing to his family by showing **love and adoration to God** for choosing him as the king of Israel. Even as his wife Michal showed contempt for his "undignified" expression of gratitude as he leaped and danced before the Lord and uncovered himself. The Bible tells us in (2 Samuel 6:14-23), not only did David bless his family but all the people of Israel by **giving** them a cake of bread, a good piece of flesh and a flagon of wine.

This sounds like a man with a multitude of resources who had a generous heart for his family and his people. No wonder he was known as a **"man after God's own heart."** David was also known to be a man of great repentance. When we see others turn from their wrongdoing, it encourages us to do the same.

David confessed and repented of his sin of adultery with Bathsheba after being confronted by Nathan the prophet. God forgave him and blessed him with another son after his first son had to die as a consequence.

Read verses: {(Psalm 51), (2 Samuel 11-12), (1 John 1:9).}

F^1 = FAMILY: God Blesses The Family
How is the Family Blessed with a Brother?

David was also a blessing to his family by being an example of forgiveness. David not only forgave Saul for trying to kill him, but he also forgave his son Absalom for his rebellion and plans to kill him. When Saul pursued David and his men, he had an opportunity to kill Saul, but he spared his life. (1 Samuel 24:1-22) David's son Absalom made plans to kill him which for many people seems unforgiveable. Often times, in our own family relationships, we find it hard to forgive minor or major offenses. I think we do this because we want to avoid repeating and experiencing the pain of the offense. We are reminded in (Colossians 3:13) to "Make allowances for each other's faults and forgive anyone who offends you. Remember, the Lord forgave you, so you must forgive others." David is an example to families that it is vital to forgive. Even though David did not have an opportunity to confront or offer to forgive his son face to face, his instructions to his men to "deal gently with young Absalom" was an indication that he loved and forgave his son. Absalom's rebellion against David the King resulted in his murder by Joab's ten armor bearers. David also forgave Shimei (who cursed the Lord's anointed) by sparing his life.

Scripture References: {(2 Samuel 15-19), (Matthew 6:14-15).}
Read more about David's character in {(1 Samuel 16-1 Kings 2).}

F¹ = FAMILY: God Blesses The Family
How is the Family Blessed with a Brother?

Reflection Activity

1. In your role as a brother, how have you been a blessing to your family? (In relation to your siblings)

_____
_____
_____
_____

2. What are some things you can do to improve in your role as a brother?

_____
_____
_____
_____

3. What do you need God to help you do?

_____
_____
_____

F^1 = FAMILY: God Blesses The Family
How is the Family Blessed with a Sister?

As I reflect upon my role as a sister, there were many highs and lows, but my goal will be to share with you the sister as a blessing to her siblings and mother. I became a sister in 1963 after being born after two (2) older brothers. I would hope I was a blessing to my brothers as I had to cook and clean when my mother had to work. As a sister of three brothers, my mother relied on me as a look-out so to speak. She never asked me to be a look-out but as a daughter, I felt it was my duty to report to her if my brothers left the house when they were told not to. I was later blessed with a younger brother in 1964 and a sister in 1974.

I was not the perfect sister as none of us are and I would be the first to tell you about all my shortcomings! I believe I was a blessing to my brothers by helping with chores. There were times when my second brother did not want to do his chores and he would offer me money to do his chores for a week. I jumped at the opportunity. I am sure the money was an incentive. As I matured, I hope that sharing my prayers and faith with my brothers was considered by them to be a blessing.

F^1 = FAMILY: God Blesses The Family
How is the Family Blessed with a Sister?

My sister was born when I was eleven (11) years old, so we did not have much in common at first because of the age difference.

My mother taught me how to take care of her because we all had to assist in her care when my mother went to work. Sisters can be a blessing to their younger siblings by aiding in their care and being a positive example to them. They can also be playmates and a teacher figure in their early learning. As my sister grew older after I left for college in 1980 (when she was six (6) years old), the distance grew between us, and I missed a lot of time watching her grow.

We began to connect again after she became a young adult and began to experience life and we would talk about life issues and share our prayers and faith. I remember once she said she was glad I would correct her when she was wrong and would share the Word and prayers with her. Well, little did she know, I would urge her to do the same for me. Sisters can be friends, confidants, prayer partners, fasting partners, accountability partners, babysitters and helpful with each other's needs, etc. I thank God for my sister because she has been a blessing to my family since my marriage in 1988. She has been kind and extremely generous with her gifts to me and my family and I often tell her she will become rich because of her generosity.

In consideration of my blended family, I must also mention that I have a sister on my Dad's side. She blesses me with her live posts on Facebook as she is so transparent which is a blessing to a lot of people. I also have two bonus sisters from my Dad's 2nd marriage, one of which I spent time with while growing up, and we have blessed each other through our past Facebook interactions and sporadic text messages and she blessed me with her presence at our brother's funeral.

F^1 = FAMILY: God Blesses The Family
How is the Family Blessed with a Sister?

There are a few sisters from the Bible that come to mind, and they are Mary (the sister or Martha and Lazarus) and Miriam (the sister of Moses and Aaron). Mary's story is familiar in the Bible because she sat at the feet of Jesus as her sister Martha was distracted by the big dinner she prepared as Jesus paid them a visit. Most women would agree they would be genuinely concerned with their house and the meal if they knew Jesus was going to visit their home.

Mary was an example of how to set our priorities in our home. This is a blessing to the family because we observe each other's behavior and will often emulate each other. Yes, there will always be chores like cleaning and cooking but there comes a time when we have to "be still " in the Lord's presence in order to be restored by His refreshing and redemptive words.

As Jesus told His disciples, they would always have the poor among them, but He would not always be physically among them and to seize the moment to spend time with Him and to offer Him a great sacrifice which for us today is not always money but also includes our time.

References: (Matthew 26:6-13) (Luke 10:38-42).

F^1 = FAMILY: God Blesses The Family
How is the Family Blessed with a Sister?

Moses and Aaron had an older sister named Miriam. She is introduced to us in (Exodus 2:1-10). Miriam's brother Moses was born at a time when the king had issued an order to the mid-wives that all male children should be killed because he feared the rapid growth of the Hebrews made the Egyptians inferior and would soon cause the Hebrews to join forces with the Egyptian enemies to fight against them and eventually escape from slavery. (Exodus 1:6-22) The midwives feared God and did not kill the baby boys but after the king reprimanded them, they told him the Hebrew women were strong and gave birth quickly and they could not get to them in time (That was a lie). The Bible commentary suggests the Lord blessed the midwives not because of the lie, but because they spared innocent lives. This leads us to Miriam's brother Moses being born. His mother Jochebed saw something special in him and decided to hide him for three (3) months but after she could no longer hide him, she waterproofed a basket to put him in and placed it in the Nile river in hopes of keeping him safe. Miriam was Moses's older sister and her actions showed that she loved him and was overprotective in the way she watched him float upon the river and was then discovered by the king's daughter.

F^1 = FAMILY: God Blesses The Family
How is the Family Blessed with a Sister?

The Bible commentary suggests the princess was barren and could not have children of her own, therefore she adopted Moses as her own son. With Miriam being a quick thinker, she devised a plan for Moses to be nursed by his own mother after she confronted the princess to ask if she wanted her to find a Hebrew woman to nurse Moses.

Not only was Miriam a blessing to her brother Moses by intervening on his behalf to provide for his physical needs but she was also providing money to her family because the princess offered to pay her for seeking a Hebrew woman to nurse Moses. Even though Moses's mother had to return Moses to the princess after he was older, his life was spared regardless, and Moses grew up in the palace as a son of the princess as a result of God using Miriam as a vessel of protection for her brother Moses. God had a greater plan for Moses! What a blessing! Along with being "overprotective," older sisters can also be a little on the "bossy" side. Speaking of "bossy," allow me to reminisce as I quote my baby brother, (God rest his soul), who wrote in my high school yearbook in 1980. He wrote:

"To Lynn, a sister who I love very much. But she is always on my case. But to tell you the truth, I cannot do without her. She keeps me going every day, with her fussing or with being nice to me. But she is going off to college soon, and I am going to miss her.
Love, Brother Red."

F^1 = FAMILY: God Blesses The Family
How is the Family Blessed with a Sister?

Some older brothers view their younger sister as someone who is caring and smart as in the yearbook inscription from my oldest brother (God rest his soul). He wrote:
"To Lynn: the only sister that really cares about her family household. Stay smart and don't have no babies. The Cain"
He viewed me as a dependable homemaker for the family who was smart, but he also warned me about what could happen if I didn't stay smart.

My second oldest brother viewed me as a mean, sweet, admirable sister who had the potential to be successful.
He wrote in my high school yearbook:
"To Linnie, a mean, sweet, little sister of mines. Keep your head straight go ahead on to school and you will have a future. Watch them little boys because they are just about the same...full of play. I will always admire you and I am sure you will have success in the future.
　　　Love ya always, bro Neil."

Miriam was older than her brother Moses, however, God had a greater calling for him. Moses, Aaron, and Miriam were all instrumental in Israel's deliverance from Egypt and neither had a cause for jealousy or envy. Don't allow your sibling's calling to interfere with yours.

F^1 = FAMILY: God Blesses The Family
How is the Family Blessed with a Sister?

Many people may not know about Miriam's role in the deliverance of Israel alongside her brothers Moses and Aaron. She was referred to as a **prophetess** in (Exodus 15:20-21) which reveals that God spoke to her as well and had a special work for her to do. (Numbers 12:1-10) She was also a **worship leader** after God delivered the Children of Israel by singing and playing her timbrel. She was also an example of how **not** to criticize or complain against those whom God has called as she did her brother Moses, however he forgave her by asking God to heal her leprosy which was her punishment for doing so. Allow God to use you and your siblings for His Kingdom. God is no respecter of persons and can use anyone who is willing to be used for His glory. Don't allow envy or jealousy to cause you to compare yourself or your gifts to anyone else. God made us each uniquely in His image and likeness, therefore, we should never try to measure up with anyone except God. His Son Jesus is our example of who to be and how to behave on this earth. It is okay to look up to your siblings (young or old) but never put them on a pedestal above God who is supreme over all beings. God gives each of us spiritual gifts to be used for His Kingdom, and not for competition or comparison.

Read the verses below for more on spiritual gifts
  {(Romans 12:6-8), (1 Corinthians 12:4-11, 28), and (Ephesians 4:11).}

F¹ = FAMILY: God Blesses The Family
How is the Family Blessed with a Sister?

Reflection Activity

1. In your role as a sister, how have you been a blessing to your family? (In relation to your siblings)

_____
_____
_____
_____

2. What are some things you can do to improve in your role as a sister?

_____
_____
_____
_____

3. What do you need God to help you do?

_____
_____

F^1 = FAMILY: God Blesses The Family
How is the Family Blessed with Brothers and Sisters

Speaking of brothers and sisters, I was reminded of a conversation Jesus had when someone told Him His mother and brothers were outside waiting to speak to Him and He asked who his mother and brothers were? Of course, Jesus knew who His natural mother and brothers were.

References: {(Matthew 1:16), (Matthew 13:55), (John 2:12).} In fact, they are mentioned by name in the Bible, and He even had sisters, even though they were not mentioned by name as his brothers. Jesus was not underestimating the value of His family but He wanted us to know the value of the spiritual family and He answered His own question by telling the people that anyone who does the will of the Father is His mother, brother, and sister. By faith, we are brothers and sisters in Christ and we are all in the Family of God. After being a member of my church for more than twenty years, I have been blessed with a number of brothers and sisters in the Body of Christ. References: {(1 Corinthians 12:27), (Hebrews 2:11), (Romans 8:29), (Matthew 12-49-50), (Mark 6:3).} We are blessed each week to receive the Word of God and to offer praises to God and to serve one another in love.

F^1 = FAMILY: God Blesses The Family
How is the Family Blessed with Brothers and Sisters

Without a shadow of a doubt, my brothers and sisters in Christ have ALL been a blessing to me by praying for me, giving me warm smiles and affectionate hugs, texting or calling to check on me, texting birthday and anniversary wishes, along with Mother's Day, Thanksgiving and Christmas text messages, sending me sermon notes, making a recording of the sermon in my absence, participating in our shared personal events (i.e. baby showers, weddings, graduations, etc.) and church programs, sending me cards and gifts for special occasions (and just because). Being in the family of God allows us to be vulnerable with each other as we have often expressed our emotions during services (i.e., crying tears of sadness or joy, crying out to God with a loud voice seeking His deliverance or offering Him praise, etc.). During these times, we can encourage each other with a smile or a hug. (Hebrews 10:24-25) Sometimes, words are not necessary as the smile and hug will say it all. Being in the family of God helps us to be accountable to each other especially when we are missing in our services or behaving in a way that is unbecoming for a child of God.
{(There is NO condemnation intended). (Romans 8:1-2)} Get connected with your brothers and sisters in Christ and be a blessing!

F^1 = FAMILY: God Blesses The Family
How is the Family Blessed with Brothers and Sisters

Reflection Activity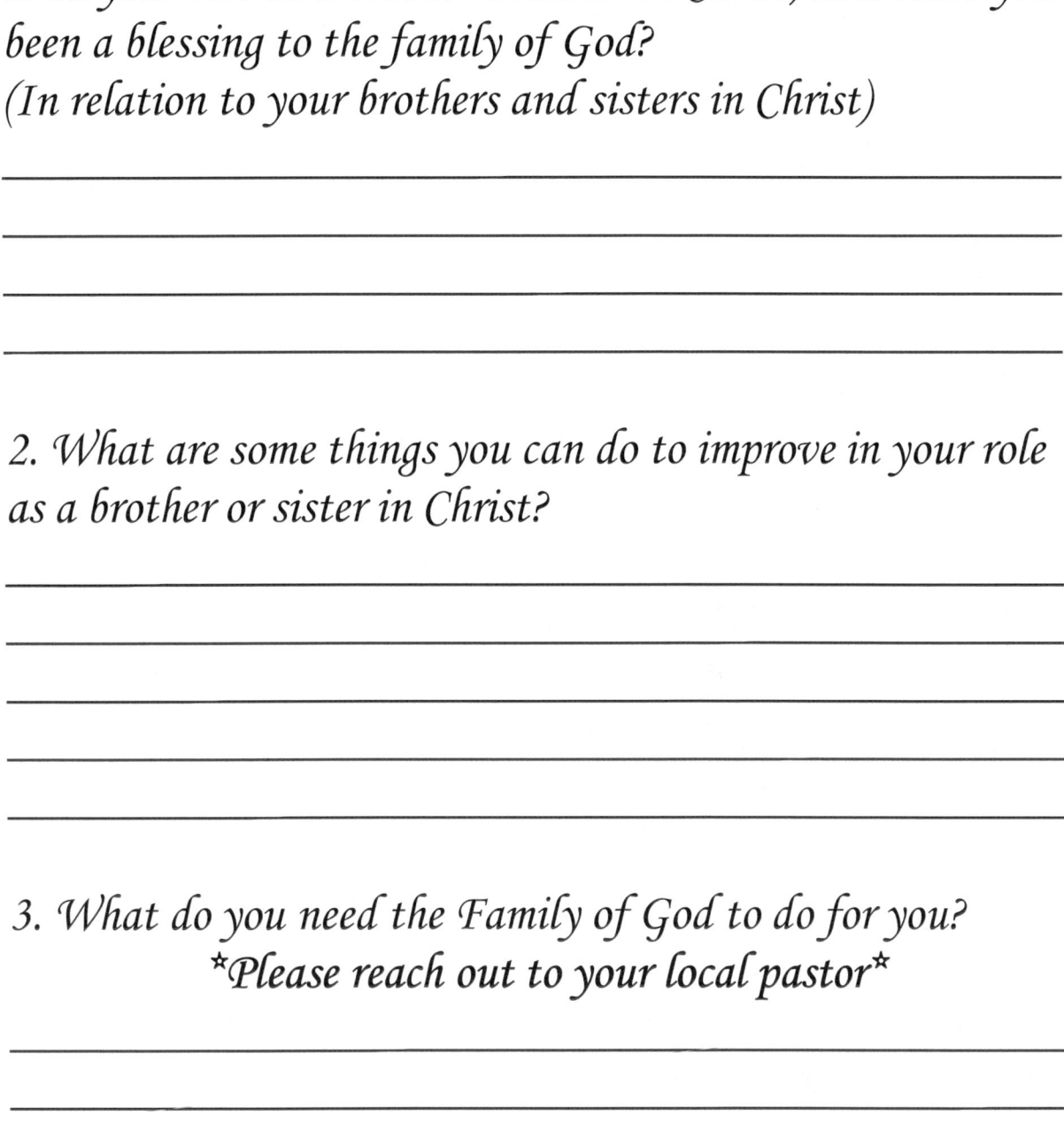

1. In your role as a brother or sister in Christ, how have you been a blessing to the family of God?
(In relation to your brothers and sisters in Christ)

_____
_____
_____
_____

2. What are some things you can do to improve in your role as a brother or sister in Christ?

_____
_____
_____
_____

3. What do you need the Family of God to do for you?
Please reach out to your local pastor

_____
_____

F^1 = FAMILY: God Blesses The Family
How is the Family Blessed with a Father-in-Law?

When I think of my father-in-law, this description comes to mind: "A hard-working man who loved his family." He was kind and always giving, especially to the kids in the family. My recollection of a Biblical father-in-law would be Jethro, (aka: Reuel). He was mentioned earlier as Moses's father-in-law. First and foremost, Jethro was a blessing to his family because he recognized that **God is greater** than any other god. (Exodus 18:11) He had heard about everything God had done for the Children of Israel by bringing them out of bondage from Egypt. (Exodus 18:9) Our **faith in God's work** and sovereignty is a blessing to our families. Jethro was also a blessing to his family by **offering practical advice** to his son-in-law Moses during one of his visits to return his daughter Zipporah (Moses's wife) who had been staying with him for a while along with her two (2) sons.

After Jethro and Moses played catch-up by sharing how things had been going, Jethro could see from Moses's workload that he was doing too much and needed to delegate more responsibility to the men of God working with him. Jethro offered a **word of advice** to Moses in specific ways but what caught my attention was that he told Moses "may God be with you" as he offered the advice. In other words, he offered the advice, but he knew that only God could empower Moses with Godly wisdom. (Exodus 18:1-27)

F^1 = FAMILY: God Blesses The Family
How is the Family Blessed with a Father-in-Law?

Reflection Activity

1. In your role as a father-in-law, how have you been a blessing to your family? (In relation to your children's spouses)

_____
_____
_____
_____

2. What are some things you can do to improve in your role as a father-in-law?

_____
_____
_____
_____

3. What do you need God to help you do?

_____
_____
_____

F^1 = FAMILY: God Blesses The Family
How is the Family Blessed with a Mother-in-Law?

The blessings that stand out about my mother-in-law (aka: mother-in-love) is that she was a great *cook, seamstress, gardener, mother, and wife*. My children used to always look forward to her neck bones. My favorite meal she prepared was baked chicken, collard greens and candied yams.

I remember when my children were toddlers, she made them pillows to sleep on as well as a white dress for my daughter. She planted and harvested all kinds of vegetables.

I believe one of my husband's favorites was the red tomato. He could eat it right from the garden. She loved all her children and grand and great-grandchildren. She was a devoted wife who showed love, respect, and gentleness to her husband. She was a praying woman of God who loved His word and His people. She would break out in a song of spontaneous worship which was an indication she loved praising the Lord and being in his presence. She served faithfully as an usher at her church. She could wear a hat like no other woman I know and was always dressed nice at church. She was a beautiful woman from the inside out. She reminded me of the virtuous woman the Bible speaks about in (Proverbs 31:10-28).

F¹ = FAMILY: God Blesses The Family
How is the Family Blessed with a Mother-in-Law?

(Proverbs 31:10-28)

...¹⁰Who can find a virtuous and capable wife?
She is more precious than rubies. ¹¹ Her husband can trust her,
and she will greatly enrich his life. ¹² She brings him good, not harm,
all the days of her life. ¹³ She finds wool and flax and busily spins it.
¹⁴ She is like a merchant's ship, bringing her food from afar.
¹⁵ She gets up before dawn to prepare breakfast for her household
and plan the day's work for her servant girls. ¹⁶ She goes to inspect a field and buys it; with her earnings she plants a vineyard.
¹⁷ She is energetic and strong, a hard worker.
¹⁸ She makes sure her dealings are profitable;
her lamp burns late into the night.
¹⁹ Her hands are busy spinning thread, her fingers twisting fiber.
²⁰ She extends a helping hand to the poor and opens her arms to the needy.
²¹ She has no fear of winter for her household,
for everyone has warm clothes. ²² She makes her own bedspreads.
She dresses in fine linen and purple gowns.
²³ Her husband is well known at the city gates, where he sits with the other civic leaders. ²⁴ She makes belted linen garments
and sashes to sell to the merchants. ²⁵ She is clothed with strength and dignity, and she laughs without fear of the future.
²⁶ When she speaks, her words are wise, and she gives instructions with kindness. ²⁷ She carefully watches everything in her household
and suffers nothing from laziness. ²⁸ Her children stand and bless her.
Her husband praises her:

F^1 = FAMILY: God Blesses The Family
How is the Family Blessed with a Mother-in-Law?

Reflection Activity

1. In your role as a mother-in-law, how have you been a blessing to your family? (In relation to your children's spouses)

___
___
___
___
___

2. What are some things you can do to improve in your role as a mother-in-law?

___
___
___
___
___

3. What do you need God to help you do?

___
___
___

F^1 = FAMILY: God Blesses The Family
How is the Family Blessed with a Son-in-law?

On July 10, 2021, my husband and I were blessed with a son-in-law, or so I like to call him my "son-in-LOVE!" Indulge me just a little to allow me to share the story behind the title "son-in-LOVE."

Many years ago, my girlfriend of forty plus years (40+) (God rest her soul) shared with me why she referred to her daughter-in-law as "daughter-in-LOVE". The story was quite profound. She told me that even though things did not work out with her son and the "daughter-in-law," as a result of a divorce, she would always love her as a daughter. Years later, when my daughter got married, I began to refer to her husband as my "son-in-LOVE."

What makes this story even more profound is the Lord gave me the revelation that the "law" can be broken but "LOVE" lasts forever. So, as I refer to my daughter's husband as my "son-in-LOVE," I am declaring that his love for my daughter is FOREVER (1 Corinthians 13:4-8)!

My "son-in-LOVE" has been a blessing to our family because he loves our daughter, he has helped my husband with lawnmower and truck cover repairs/installation, and he sends us the sweetest videos of our granddaughter!

F^1 = FAMILY: God Blesses The Family
How is the Family Blessed with a Son-in-law?

My "son-in-LOVE" also blesses our family by being a *conversational companion* to my husband when we visit each other because they have a lot in common as they both commentate sports. The two of them can give you all the latest updates or changes with the players and even foresee changes that have not already occurred.

When I am in the kitchen cooking and my husband is outside grilling, I can call on him to empty the trash or to pick up last-minute items from the store. He usually says something funny to make me laugh or make me want to pop him which I never do, at least not with the intention of harming him. Just an endearing touch to let him know I love him.

He blesses me when I see him cry or lift his hands or voice in worship because that is something we have in common.
There is just something about a man crying and praising God that touches me deep in my heart. ♡

He blessed me as he would FaceTime or send a video to show me the latest venture of my granddaughter standing on her own or driving her new Bentley she received on her second birthday!

F^1 = FAMILY: God Blesses The Family
How is the Family Blessed with a Son-in-law?

Before Jacob became the **son-in-law** of Laban {(who was also Jacob's mother Rebekah's brother which made him Jacob's uncle)}, he was introduced as his uncle. Jacob became a prospective son-in-law for Laban as an answer to his father Isaac's prayer for God to bless him with one of his uncle's daughters as a wife. Jacob did as his father asked him to do by going to Paddan-aram to choose a wife and not to marry a Canaanite woman who worshipped idol gods. Jacob was brought to tears as he met Laban's daughter Rachel at the well and assisted her with watering the flocks. I conclude that he was brought to tears because he met the woman his father Isaac had described to him before he left home. Jacob is described in the Bible as a "deceiver," however in this instance he can be viewed as a blessed example of obedience to the family. He can also be viewed as a man of **hard work** and integrity as he interacted with Rachel at the well which I am sure her father thought was commendable. *(Genesis 29:1-30)* Jacob was also **obedient** as he was **willing to follow customs** offering dowry to the prospective bride's family, however, since he didn't have anything, he was willing to work for a total of fourteen (14) years for the love of his life who was Rachel. You must read the rest of Jacob's story as it is told in *(Genesis 25-50)*.

F^1 = FAMILY: God Blesses The Family
How is the Family Blessed with a Son-in-Law?

Reflection Activity

1. In your role as a son-in-law, how have you been a blessing to your family? (In relation to your spouse's parents)

_____
_____
_____
_____
_____

2. What are some things you can do to improve in your role as a son-in-law?

_____
_____
_____
_____
_____

3. What do you need God to help you do?

_____
_____
_____

F¹= FAMILY: God Blesses The Family
How is the Family Blessed with a Daughter-in-law?

A woman becomes a "daughter-in-law" when she marries a couple's son. I can think of four women in my personal life who have only one son, two of which have gained a "bonus" daughter by their son's marriage. Many view marriage as a form of "interference" and "division" in the parent-child relationship. However, if we would just take a step back and analyze the situation as a whole, we would find that daughters-in-law can be a true blessing to the family.

References: {(Genesis 2:24), (Matthew 19:5), Mark 10:7).} Naomi's daughter-in-law Ruth is a well-known daughter-in-law of the Bible. Naomi and her husband Elimelech moved to Moab with their family because of the famine. After Naomi's husband died, she was left with her two (2) sons, Kilion and Mahlon. Both her sons married Moabite women and Ruth and her sister-in-law Orpah was their names. Ruth married Mahlon and Orpah married Kilion. Ten years later, both the sons died leaving Ruth with her mother-in-law Naomi and her sister-in-law Orpah as widows. Their predicament caused them to return to Judah because they heard the famine was over. Ruth's mother-in-law Naomi tried to convince her to return to her country in hopes of gaining another marriage. Orpah returned while Ruth refused to leave her mother-in-law's side. She was an example of love and faithfulness in this relationship.

F¹= FAMILY: God Blesses The Family
How is the Family Blessed with a Daughter-in-law?

Ruth was also an **example of faith and courage** to return to a land that despised her people. She was committed to **worship the one TRUE God** and to remain with her mother-in-law's people. She risked being a poor widow returning to Judah without resources or a husband, but Ruth trusted this new God in which she had taken refuge. Ruth was **willing to go to work** in the fields to gather leftover grain to **provide for** herself and her mother-in-law. Her **work** ethic was so admirable, Boaz noticed her. He was the (2nd in line) kinsman redeemer who made sure she had lunch, water, safety, and extra grain enough to share with her mother-in-law. According to www.gotquestions.org, the kinsman-redeemer is a male relative who, {according to various laws of the Pentateuch (first five (5) books of the Bible)}, had the privilege or responsibility to act on behalf of a relative who was in trouble, danger, or need. (Ruth 2:8-9, 14, 17-19)

Boaz told Ruth: "I've been told all about what you have done for your mother-in-law since the death of your husband." (Ruth 2:11) Ruth was **respectful** and **obedient** by following the advice (Ruth 3:5-6) of her mother-in-law to approach the kinsman redeemer, (Ruth 3-4) which put her in position to marry Boaz and have a son, Obed (who was the father of Jesse and grandfather of David) to carry on her dead husband's name and to keep the family's land. Ruth is referred to as being better to her mother-in-law than seven (7) sons. (Ruth 4:15) Ruth's story is significant in that her faithful obedience prepared for the coming of the promised Messiah, Jesus Christ.

F¹= FAMILY: God Blesses The Family
How is the Family Blessed with a Daughter-in-Law?

Reflection Activity

1. In your role as a daughter-in-law, how have you been a blessing to your family? (In relation to your spouse's parents)

_____
_____
_____
_____
_____

2. What are some things you can do to improve in your role as a daughter-in-law?

_____
_____
_____
_____
_____

3. What do you need God to help you do?

_____
_____
_____

F^1 = FAMILY: God Blesses The Family
How is the Family Blessed with a Brother-in-law?

As I examine my personal life, I have reaped some benefits of having a brother-in-law or so I like to call them "brother-in-love." On my side of the family, I only have one brother-in-love who I will always love for his **respect** towards me as a sister, **sharing career insights** with my children and the consistency in our relationship over the years. However, on my husband's side of the family, I have six (6) brothers-in-love. My oldest "brother-in-love" was full of **laughter.**

No matter what he spoke about, he could always find a way to laugh. That is what I remember most about him, God rest his soul.

My second oldest brother-in-love is **quite the mechanic.**

He often helps my husband trouble-shoot issues with cars, trucks, sports utility vehicles, (aka: SUV's), motorcycles, Can-Am "Spyders," and just about anything that has a wheel or motor. He also **prays powerful and effective prayers** during our church services which blesses my soul.

My third oldest brother-in-love was a minister of the gospel and he used to bless my soul as he **preached the Word and prayed from his heart.** He had quite the sense of humor and made us laugh. God rest his soul. A person who can make you laugh, can ultimately *inspire joy.* The joy of the Lord is our strength. (Nehemiah 8:10)

F¹= FAMILY: God Blesses The Family
How is the Family Blessed with a Brother-in-law?

My fourth oldest brother-in-love was one who **persevered** in the midst of struggle and always stood up for his rights. God rest his soul.

My sixth brother-in-love closest to my husband's age is very **humble**. I have never heard him speak a harsh word or see him stressed about anything.

My youngest brother-in-love is quite the **helper** to my husband as well. He often meets him at the church to work on projects and to be a second pair of eyes and hands. He is an impressive **teacher of the Word of God** and can always **make you laugh**.

There is one brother-in-law referred to in the Bible who had quite the essentiality in the family. In (Deuteronomy 25:5-6), we are told: ⁵ "If two brothers are living together on the same property and one of them dies without a son, his widow may not be married to anyone from outside the family. Instead, her husband's brother should marry her and have intercourse with her to fulfill the duties of a brother-in-law. ⁶ The first son she bears to him will be considered the son of the dead brother, so that his name will not be forgotten in Israel."

This is an example of a Levirate marriage, and it literally means a "marriage with a brother-in-law." It has nothing to do with the tribe of Levi. The purpose for this type of marriage was to preserve the family name and inheritance! (www.gotquestions.org)

F¹ = FAMILY: God Blesses The Family
How is the Family Blessed with a Brother-in-Law?

Reflection Activity

1. In your role as a brother-in-law, how have you been a blessing to your family? (In relation to your sibling's spouses)

_____
_____
_____
_____
_____

2. What are some things you can do to improve in your role as a brother-in-law?

_____
_____
_____
_____
_____

3. What do you need God to help you do?

_____
_____
_____

F^1 = FAMILY: God Blesses The Family
How is the Family Blessed with a Sister-in-law?

My husband's side of the family has afforded us with seven (7) sisters-in-law (aka: sisters-in-love). My oldest sister-in-love can be described as beautiful, **kind, giving and funny**. She consistently **shows love** to all her family members by sending greeting cards in the mail for birthdays, Mothers and Father's Day, Thanksgiving, Christmas, and Resurrection Day.

My second oldest sister-in-love is **a good cook**. The family enjoys her famous "hash" recipe (aka: Brunswick stew).

My third oldest sister-in-love is an **anointed seamstress** and **decorator** who made just about all my masks to wear during Covid-19 and made wreaths to adorn our doors at Christmas and a mailbox décor for my daughter's wedding.

My fourth oldest sister-in-love has a **smile** that can lighten any room she enters and she is **gentle and kind** to everyone in her presence.

My fifth oldest sister-in-love is an example of **perseverance** in her personal life and commitment to her **faith, marriage, family, and beliefs**.

F^1 = FAMILY: God Blesses The Family
How is the Family Blessed with a Sister-in-law?

My sixth oldest sister-in-love is an example of kindness and joy. She gives genuine hugs and love to her family.

My youngest sister-in-love is beautiful on the outside as well as the inside and her devotion to her husband and two daughters is commendable.

I have another sister-in-love who is married to my youngest brother-in-love and she blesses me with expert medical advice no matter the nature of my text or call. She is also a student of the Word of God and blesses me with her Sunday School reviews and might I add that she makes a delicious pound cake to share at family gatherings.

My next sister-in-love blesses me with her presence at our family gatherings and when she allows the children to come and spend time at our house. She also blesses me when she invites me to her family Bible Study sessions.

Last, but not least, another sister-in-love blesses me with her spontaneous phone calls and she makes the best mac and cheese to share at our family gatherings.

F¹= FAMILY: God Blesses The Family
How is the Family Blessed with a Sister-in-Law?

Reflection Activity

1. In your role as a sister-in-law, how have you been a blessing to your family? (In relation to your sibling's spouses)

_____
_____
_____
_____
_____

2. What are some things you can do to improve in your role as a sister-in-law?

_____
_____
_____
_____
_____

3. What do you need God to help you do?

_____
_____
_____

F^1 = FAMILY: God Blesses The Family
How is the Family Blessed with a Grandmother?

My maternal grandmother was a blessing to my family because she showed us **genuine love** and affection. She was also a woman of **wisdom**. One of her favorite sayings was that "**God is too wise to make a mistake and too just to do wrong.**" That phrase has remained with me for over fifty (50) years. She loved the Lord and shared her faith. She was a dedicated member of her church and received accolades on her job for her ability to cook. She taught my mother how to make homemade biscuits and my mother taught me, and I taught my daughter. When she entered your presence, there was always a hug and a kiss. One vivid memory of my grandmother was when she was in her 80's, she used to call to check up on me and my family and she would send us letters and cash in the mail for our birthdays. That was a real love offering.

My paternal grandmother was a great cook as well and was an entrepreneur, which was praiseworthy back in the 60's and 70's. One of the things I remember about the family store was that she would give us butter cookies and pickled pig feet. We would eat so many pig feet, our lips would be white from the vinegar. She was **generous and kind** to her family and neighbors. These two women left a legacy for their families and remind me of the (Proverbs 31) woman.

F¹= FAMILY: God Blesses The Family
How is the Family Blessed with a Grandmother?

Now that I have shared my grandmothers, and how they were a blessing to their families, let's explore one of our Biblical grandmothers who is only mentioned by name once in a verse (2 Timothy 1:5) but apparently she had a major impact on her grandson Timothy's life. Her name was Lois, and she is referred to as having **"unfeigned"** faith which Paul could see in Timothy (his son in the ministry) as he was referred to in the Bible. This **"unfeigned"** faith meant that their faith was undissembled (not pretended but genuine) and sincere. Sometimes we need a reminder of the faith our grandparents had in the Lord and how it was their faith that enabled them to persevere and to overcome prejudice and injustice. Paul was the person who reminded Timothy of his grandmother Lois's faith which came at a much-needed time when he was facing the fear of opposition, persecution, and rejection when he was given the task to oversee the young church in Ephesus.
(1 Timothy 1:3-5)

I was told by one of my family members that because of their grandmother's prayers, they overcame a lot of adversity and rebellion in their life and because they were reassured their grandmother would continue to pray, they turned from their youthful mischief. Thank God for grandmothers!

F^1 = FAMILY: God Blesses The Family
How is the Family Blessed with a Grandmother?

Reflection Activity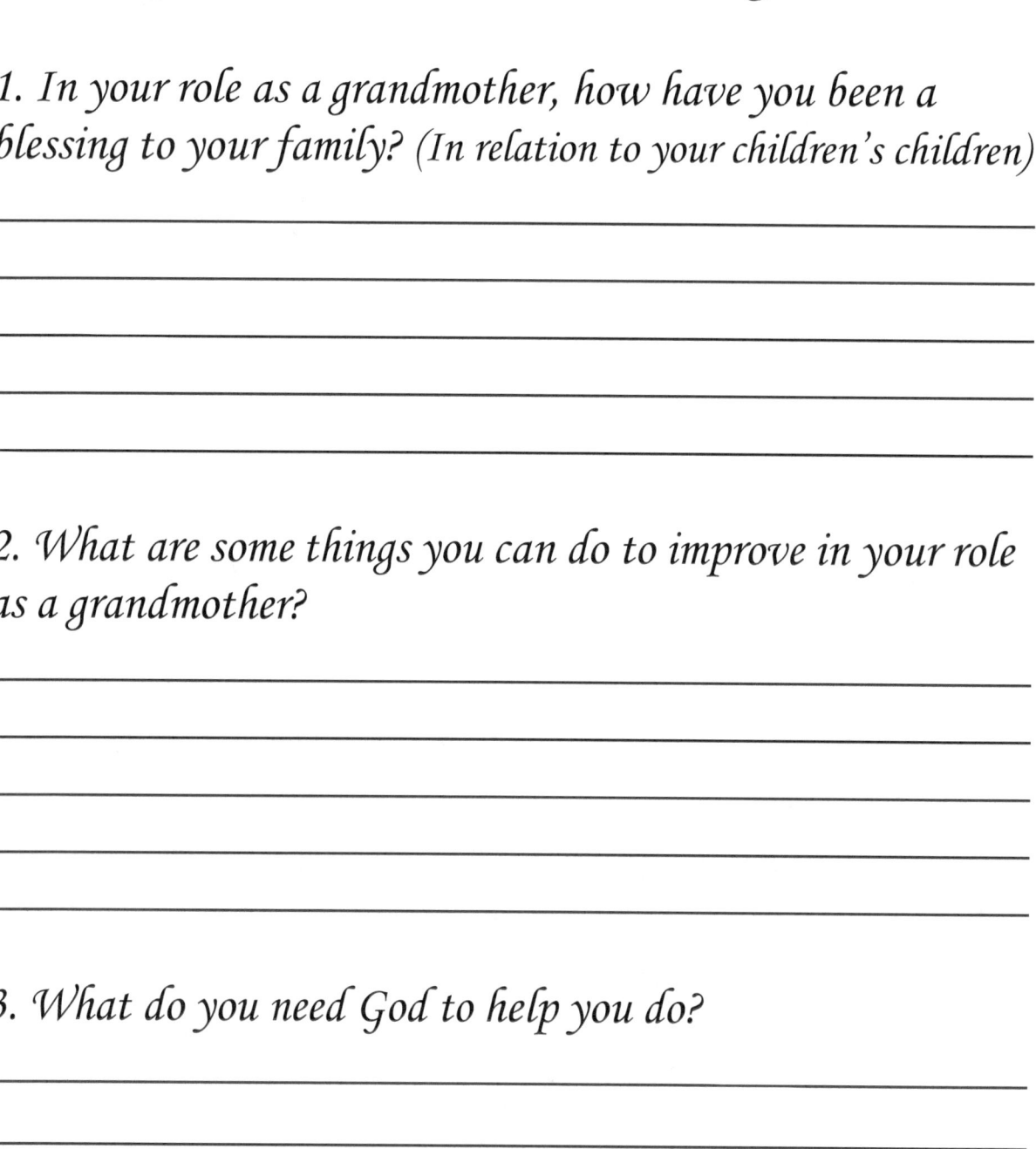

1. *In your role as a grandmother, how have you been a blessing to your family? (In relation to your children's children)*

___
___
___
___
___

2. *What are some things you can do to improve in your role as a grandmother?*

___
___
___
___
___

3. *What do you need God to help you do?*

___
___
___

F¹ = FAMILY: God Blesses The Family
How is the Family Blessed with a Grandfather?

*It is unfortunate that I did not get to meet my maternal grandfather; however, my paternal grandfather was a **hard-working** businessman who provided for his family and was a strict **disciplinarian** whenever necessary. I should know because he "tore my butt up" for a misunderstanding between me and my cousin. Even though I was not at fault, it was the result of the disciplinary action. I remember how he used to care for the pigs and plant crops like sugar cane and made homemade syrup. Another picturesque moment of him was whenever my grandmother would cook greens, he would get a fresh onion and slice it to put over his greens.*

The Bible mentions grandchildren as "children's children" and how they are blessed by their grandparents.

*A grandfather who **fears the Lord** and is faithful and **obedient to God**, has salvation extended to his "children's children" (aka: grandchildren). (Psalm 103:17-18)*

*Good people leave an **inheritance** to their grandchildren, but the sinners wealth passes to the godly. (Proverbs 13:22)*

Even though physical inheritance (i.e., land, money, and other material blessings) is just as important now as it was in the Bible, the most important inheritance a grandfather can leave to his grandchildren is a spiritual inheritance.

F¹ = FAMILY: God Blesses The Family
How is the Family Blessed with a Grandfather?

How does a grandfather bless his grandchildren with a spiritual inheritance? Be the kind of grandfather who stores up treasures in heaven and not store up treasures on earth, only to pass away and not get to enjoy it or eternal life as the rich fool did in the Bible. (Luke 12:13-21)

How does a grandfather store up treasures in heaven?

Doing this goes far beyond **paying tithes**. Paying tithes is great for the work of the church and the Kingdom but that is not all God requires of the believer. (Malachi 3:10) (Matthew 6:19-20)

God requires the believer to be **obedient** and to fulfill all the purposes He has set for the believer. (1 Samuel 15:22)

Another way a grandfather stores up treasures in heaven is to **work hard as if he is working for the Lord** and not men and he will receive his inheritance. (Colossians 3:23-24) Helping the poor is another example of storing up treasures in heaven because when we do, we are lending to the Lord and He will repay. (Proverbs 19:17) But be careful to check your motives and do not help others expecting something in return. Your reward is in heaven. Be careful not to love your money more than God (Matthew 19:16-22) and study God's Word so that He may approve you and know that your labor in the Lord is not in vain.

Read verses: {(2 Timothy 2:15), (1 Corinthians 15:58).}

F¹ = FAMILY: God Blesses The Family
How is the Family Blessed with a Grandfather?

Reflection Activity

1. In your role as a grandfather, how have you been a blessing to your family? (In relation to your children's children)

_____
_____
_____
_____
_____

2. What are some things you can do to improve in your role as a grandfather?

_____
_____
_____
_____

3. What do you need God to help you do?

_____
_____
_____

F¹ = FAMILY: God Blesses The Family
How is the Family Blessed with an Aunt?

Your aunt is your mother or father's sister or the wife of your uncle or your grandparents sister or your spouse's aunt.

An aunt can hold a very special place in your heart. She can be a **friend** who listens and gives sound advice when you think your parents won't listen or understand. She can even be like a sister depending on your age differences and can even take on the role of a mother figure if your mama has passed away or has been estranged. My sister has played a special role in my daughter and granddaughter's lives.

In the Bible, an aunt is referred to as "mother's sister" or "father's sister." When we read (**John 19:25**), the focus would likely be on Mary Magdalene because Jesus had cast out seven (7) demons from within her, however, there was another woman (nameless) who was present at the cross during Jesus's crucifixion, and it was **Jesus's aunt** who is referred to as "his mother's sister". There was a multitude of people present at the crucifixion, however, not all of them are mentioned. I had read this verse in the past and never focused on the mention of Jesus's aunt. How many of you have an aunt who is **supportive** of your mother?

Picture this: you are watching as your nephew is being crucified and you have to stand next to his mother (your sister), to **offer support and comfort**. What could that have been like? Very difficult I would presume.

F¹ = FAMILY: God Blesses The Family
How is the Family Blessed with an Aunt?

*Speaking of supportive aunts, I remember going to my cousin's Homegoing about sixty-five miles from my house and one of my aunts was there and she was **raving about the "Obedience" book** that I wrote saying there was a verse for "everything" which really blessed me because it was a reminder that God has given us "EVERYTHING" we need pertaining to life and godliness in His WORD (2 Peter 1:3)!*

*On another occasion in February 2015, my other aunt visited a local church outside of Leesburg, Georgia to **support me** as I was the keynote speaker for a Women's Conference. She later informed me that she was so **impressed with my speaking** that she wanted me to do a "Thank-You" at her husband's Homegoing which I did in the form of an engaging presentation! She was impressed with that as well. I told her that God deserves all the praises for what He enables me to do. She also blesses me with **her calls** because it makes me feel she is thinking about me, and she loves me! She is quite funny by the way and is sure to make you laugh!*

F^1 = FAMILY: God Blesses The Family
How is the Family Blessed with an Aunt?

*I have three (3) maternal aunts who have gone on to be with the Lord. One of which I was very close to. As a teenager, I would ride my bicycle to her house to spend time with her. She was a **good listener** and always gave me **encouraging words**.* 😇

Another of these aunts was the hostess of my bridal shower. I thought it was very **hospitable** for her to open up her home for my celebration. 😇

My other aunt was a very special part of my early years by **allowing me to stay with her** while my mother was in California. She would always accommodate family. 😇

Yet another aunt would **plan the bridal shower** and also allowed me to **spend nights** with her two daughters (my cousins) and allowed me an extended stay as my Mama was in California. Even now as we are both "seasoned" adults {(as she is seventeen (17) years my senior)}, she continues to bless me with our "text conversations," not to mention she shares the best chicken Brunswick stew.

F¹= FAMILY: God Blesses The Family
How is the Family Blessed with an Aunt?

Another of my aunts inspires me with her longevity and her outlook on life as well as her fearless ability to take trips and cruises. We visited her recently and something she said was so profound and remains with me today, and it was that no matter how much we plan or think about the "what ifs," GOD IS IN CONTROL!

And last, but certainly not the least of these aunts (maternal), is the aunt who always made me feel welcome during the many visits to my grandmother's house as many of her nieces and nephews frequented grandmama's house and kitchen. She recently told me in a text that she would always love me! I reach out to her sometimes to let her know she crossed my mind and I try to text her every year on her birthday!

I would also like to mention that my aunt, who is married to my Dad's last surviving brother, was a huge blessing when she called me back in October 2021 to ask for details on how to purchase the Obedience book I published. I was humbled! And yet again, another paternal aunt blesses me with her warm smiles and her ability to get on the dance floor solo and enjoy music while dancing. It is a reminder that even in old age, we can still enjoy life and be fruitful .(Psalm 94:14)

F^1 = FAMILY: God Blesses The Family
How is the Family Blessed with an Aunt?

Let's take a look at another Biblical aunt whom you may not have ever heard of. There was a Queen of Judah named Athaliah who had a son named Ahaziah who at age 22 ascended to the throne as King. He was murdered because of his evil deeds and his mother Queen Athaliah killed his children so that she could take the throne.

Imagine a grandmother who kills her own grandchildren. Don't be quick to judge her though! We kill with our words all the time. "Unbeknownst to Athaliah, one of the grandchildren escaped with the help from **Jehosheba, the baby's aunt** (and the wife of the high priest Jehoiada), who took the infant Joash and hid him and his nurse in a bedroom. Joash was later smuggled out of the castle and taken to the temple, where he remained hidden for six years while Queen Athaliah reigned over the land (2 Kings 11:1–3). Interestingly, the name Athaliah means either **"God is exalted"** or **"dealt violently with by God."** Queen Athaliah did not exalt God with her life; instead, God dealt violently with her. After Athaliah had reigned six years, the high priest Jehoiada set guards around the temple and publicly crowned the young Joash as the rightful king. As the new king was anointed, "the people clapped their hands and shouted, 'Long live the king!'" (2 Kings 11:12).

F¹ = FAMILY: God Blesses The Family
How is the Family Blessed with an Aunt?

"Queen Athaliah heard the commotion, realized what was happening, and ran out of the palace shouting, "Treason! Treason!" (verse 13). Jehoiada commanded the troops to capture Athaliah and execute her, so they killed the queen "where the horses enter the palace grounds" (verse 16). "Seven-year-old King Joash, under the direction of the faithful high priest, tore down the temple of Baal, smashed the altars and images of Baal, and killed the priest of Baal. And "all the people of the land rejoiced, and the city was calm, because Athaliah had been slain" (verse 20) www.gotquestions.org. Had it not been for King Joash's **aunt (Jehosheba)** and her bravery, he would have been killed along with his siblings. God had a plan for Joash. He was king of Judah for forty (40) years. He depended on the advice of the priest and other leaders. His knowledge of God was based on secondhand experiences. He quoted in (2 Chronicles 24:5) "Go to all the towns of Judah and collect the required annual offerings, so that we can repair the Temple of your God. Do not delay!" He had good intentions but he never pursued a personal relationship with God. He was assassinated by his own servants because of his bad choices. How is this story relevant to us today? People can intervene in our lives but ultimately we are responsible for what we do. (Read: 2 Chronicles 24:1-27)

F¹ = FAMILY: God Blesses The Family
How is the Family Blessed with an Aunt?

Reflection Activity

1. In your role as an aunt, how have you been a blessing to your family? (In relation to your nieces and nephews)

___
___
___
___

2. What are some things you can do to improve in your role as an aunt?

___
___
___
___

3. What do you need God to help you do?

___
___

F^1 = FAMILY: God Blesses The Family
How is the Family Blessed with an Uncle?

Your uncle is your mother's or father's brother or your aunt's husband or your spouse's uncle or your grandparents uncle. Uncles can be a blessing in so many ways. Similarly to an aunt, an uncle can also hold a very special place in your heart. He can be a friend who listens and gives sound advice when you think your parents won't listen or understand. He can even be like a brother depending on your age differences. He can even take on the role of a father figure if your daddy has passed away or has been estranged.

An uncle can also be a blessing particularly by helping family members in need, (Leviticus 25:49) or being a wise counselor as David's uncle Jonathan was. (1 Chronicles 27:32) Did you know David had a friend and uncle with the same name Jonathan? Neither did I until I studied this verse. According to www.esword.net , there were four (4) Israelites with that same name.

Uncles can be very rare, and I say that literally because I only have two (2) uncles left on both sides of my family.

One of these uncles blesses the family with his support by driving his sisters around and cooking on the grill and sharing the barbeque. He also blesses me with his texts and calls along with his presence at family events. The other uncle is very funny and brings lots of laughter to the table (literally) as I discovered during our family dinner at my house.

F^1 = FAMILY: God Blesses The Family
How is the Family Blessed with an Uncle?

Reflection Activity

1. In your role as an uncle, how have you been a blessing to your family? (In relation to your nieces and nephews)

___
___
___
___

2. What are some things you can do to improve in your role as an uncle?

___
___
___
___

3. What do you need God to help you do?

___
___
___

F¹= FAMILY: God Blesses The Family
How is the Family Blessed with a Cousin?

I believe the most prominent and blessed cousin in the Bible had to be John the Baptist. He was the cousin of Jesus Christ the Messiah. He was what we call the **"forerunner"*** of Jesus Christ. (John 3:28) (*one who announces or indicates the later arrival of another)
John the Baptist and Jesus were only six (6) months apart as John the Baptist's mother Elizabeth was six months pregnant when Jesus's mother Mary discovered she would be having a baby by way of the Holy Spirit. Why was John the Baptist such a blessing to his cousin Jesus Christ?
God called him to be a blessing to Jesus directly and for His Kingdom. His conception was a miracle as a result of a prayer from his father Zechariah and he was filled with the Holy Spirit in his mother Elizabeth's womb. Read (Luke 1:1-80).

He was a blessing to Jesus and the Kingdom of God by:
- ✝ Isolating himself in the wilderness to hear from God as he was set apart for the call of God (John 1:23) (Isaiah 40:3-5)
- ✝ Acknowledging Jesus as greater than himself (John 3:30)
- ✝ Preaching repentance and people's need for God (Matthew 3:2)
- ✝ Standing up to self-righteous people (Matthew 3:7-10)
- ✝ Went to prison for the sake of Christ (Mark 6:17-20)
- ✝ Faithful to God until the day he died (Mark 6:21-28)

F^1 = FAMILY: God Blesses The Family
How is the Family Blessed with a Cousin?

As I reflect on the life of John the Baptist and how faithful he was to the cause of Christ, it makes me pose the following questions to us today: And yes, you can write in YOUR book!

- *Am I the kind of cousin who would give up a lavish lifestyle to live a simple life to fulfill my purpose in God while supporting my cousin?* _____
- *Am I the kind of cousin who would be willing to stand in the background as my cousin received the greater recognition?* _____
- *Am I the kind of cousin who will tell people they need Jesus?* _____
- *Am I the kind of cousin who is willing to go to prison for the Kingdom of God?* _____
- *Am I the kind of cousin who is willing to be put to death for the cause of Christ?* _____

If you need additional space, use the lines below:

_____
_____
_____
_____
_____

F^1 = FAMILY: God Blesses The Family
How is the Family Blessed with a Cousin?

*As I reflect on my own family, there is not enough space on these pages to discuss my cousins individually and the **blessings of all my cousins** on both sides of the family so I will attempt to sum up how they have been a blessing in my life. My cousins have been a blessing in my life by texting me scripture, texting me out of the blue just to check up on me, inviting me to their homes and sharing their food and a spare bed, hosting our "Cousin's Christmas", hosting our family gatherings and Zoom meetings, sending me birthday and anniversary greetings, catering the food at my 25th wedding anniversary celebration, inviting me to church, spending time with me at family events, sending me gifts for my retirement in 2023, surprise visits and calls when they are near Highway 300, attending my speaking engagements or supporting the family at birthday parties or funerals, etc. I am grateful for my cousins on both sides of my family because we have shared some good times over the years as well as some challenging times! I pray we continue to be a blessing to each other as we are getting older, and we are adding grandchildren and great-grandchildren to the family.*

F^1 = FAMILY: God Blesses The Family
How is the Family Blessed with a Nephew?

A nephew is your brother or sister's son or your brother or sister-in-law's son. In my small circle, I have three (3) nephews. One of which I am pretty close to. He has been a blessing to his "Auntie" as he affectionately calls me. As he has grown into a young adult and is old enough to drive and make his own decisions, he has been a blessing to me by running errands, helping to load and unload my car, meeting me to give his mother and grandmother food when I cooked and wanted to share. When he was younger, he used to spend the night with me, and we would play games and do Children's Bible Study activities. A few of his favorite things for me to cook for him are cheeseburgers, grilled cheese sandwiches with beef and vegetable soup, and before he stopped eating a lot of sweets, he enjoyed my buttermilk pies. He has the same name as my son, and I often view him as a son in the spirit.

Paul had a nephew who is referred to as "Paul's sister's son" in (Acts 23:16). Over forty people were plotting to kill Paul because of his preaching and hope in the resurrection and his nephew overheard the conversation. He was a blessing to Paul in that he was **instrumental in warning the commander** who believed (and later King Agrippa) that Paul was not deserving of imprisonment or death, and he set a plan in motion for Paul to escape. (Acts 23:6, 29; 26:31)

F¹ = FAMILY: God Blesses The Family
How is the Family Blessed with a Nephew?

My other nephew on my side of the family is close to my daughter's age and he also affectionately calls me "Aunty." Reflecting on him as a baby, he was very quiet and sweet. I try to reach out via text message, especially on his birthday. I told him we needed to be more intentional with getting in touch especially since he does not live that far from where I live. He blessed me this past April 2024 by celebrating with us at our house as we celebrated my granddaughter's second birthday!

Another one of my nephews who lives up North has been a blessing by pleasantly surprising me with his text messages and phone calls to check up on me when I had a health wakeup call back in January 2023 and when my brother passed away in March 2024. We also talk about and share healthy recipes. Might I add that he is very funny, and my husband enjoys talking to him about sports and sometimes politics.

F^1 = FAMILY: God Blesses The Family
How is the Family Blessed with a Nephew?

*Yet, another nephew comes to mind along with his wife (my niece) who are frequently giving us praises for the longevity of our marriage. When we have family gatherings in the Fall, they are **ready to help** by "juggling" my requests for help (even after having to drive from another state to attend the gathering).*

*By the way, my nephew's wife was a **great assistant hostess** by jumping in, directing traffic, and managing the flow of things (while I showered and got dressed) and she even monitored the stove as if it were her own kitchen. She stated that she knew what it was like to be a hostess for a large group. To God be the Glory for sustaining our marriage for 36 years as of 2024.*

*Several years ago, we were invited to spend Thanksgiving with family in another state and I remember preparing brunch and my younger nephew came into the kitchen **willing to help** and the older one was helpful cleaning and setting up chairs one year at our annual family gathering.*

F¹ = FAMILY: God Blesses The Family
How is the Family Blessed with a Nephew?

Reflection Activity

1. In your role as a nephew, how have you been a blessing to your family? (In relation to your aunts and uncles)

_____
_____
_____
_____

2. What are some things you can do to improve in your role as a nephew?

_____
_____
_____
_____

3. What do you need God to help you do?

_____
_____
_____

F^1 = FAMILY: God Blesses The Family
How is the Family Blessed with a Niece?

A niece is your sister or brother's daughter or your sibling's granddaughter or your spouse's niece. Thus far on my side of the family, I have one (1) niece and three (3) great nieces.

On my husband's side of the family, we have about thirteen (13) nieces.

My sister and I often speak about being committed to being "intentional" when it comes to making an effort to reach out to family members to maintain a connection. Over the past few years, I have worked to maintain a connection with my nieces on both sides of the family. I send text messages periodically to check on them to see how they are doing and to hear about their recent involvement in social activities, academic and career pursuits, and extracurricular activities. We also planned and executed a girls weekend in which we spent a couple of nights together, played games, talked, laughed, cooked, ate, and one of them even came to Christ after our group prayer. Hallelujah! I was pleasantly surprised by my nieces when they texted me on my birthday in April 2024. That brought me joy because I had been the one initiating the connection and that made me feel my efforts were well worth it.

In September 2023, one of my nieces called to ask if they could lodge with us and we gladly obliged. I prepared brunch for her as we sat on the sunporch sharing so much about our families and careers and discovered we had a lot in common.

F^1 = FAMILY: God Blesses The Family
How is the Family Blessed with a Niece?

We shared our physical challenges as well as some emotional challenges. I was fascinated to discover just how much we had in common even though I am only a little more than five (5) years her senior.

All it takes is to start a conversation and your eyes will begin to open to a new and improved relationship with your family members. She said the time away from her normal routine was exactly what she needed to refresh. I was happy my husband and I could provide her with lodging and fellowship.

Little did she know, her presence and testimonies were very inspiring and uplifting. When we share things in common with others, it encourages us to persevere in our struggles. Afterall, the Bible tells us we overcome by the Blood of the Lamb and the word of our testimony. (Revelation 12:11)

heartlight.org

F^1 = FAMILY: God Blesses The Family
How is the Family Blessed with a Niece?

Reflection Activity

1. In your role as a niece, how have you been a blessing to your family? (In relation to your aunts and uncles)
___
___
___
___
___

2. What are some things you can do to improve in your role as a niece?
___
___
___
___
___

3. What do you need God to help you do?
___
___
___

F^1 = FAMILY: God Blesses The Family
How is the Family Blessed with a Granddaughter?

Even though I am not sure how my grandmothers would have responded to this question in the subtitle, I can truly tell you how my granddaughter has been a blessing in my life and my husband's life thus far in her two (2) years in this world.

I remember the first time we met. She was only eight (8) days old, and it was love at first sight. I held her in my arms while giving her a bottle of her Mom's breast milk and I later walked her upstairs to her room to rock her to sleep but I wanted her "Papa" to hold her so I took her back downstairs for him to hold her and I could see the love and adoration on his face, even as he was wearing his mask, as we were in the midst of Covid-19 even in the year 2022. As she is growing up so fast, (as she is two years old now), she blesses us in the following ways: **her smiles** as she hears our voices and sees our faces as we are on the speaker phone or FaceTime. We began to FaceTime when she was about eleven days old however, she didn't actually start **engaging with me** until she was about six (6) weeks old. She would actually smile at me as I would talk to her. At age two, she **gives the best hugs** and will not let go until she is ready. It is adorable to hear her call me "G-Lynn" and my husband "Papa," and it melts our hearts when she blows us multiple kisses on FaceTime. That is truly a blessing!

F¹= FAMILY: God Blesses The Family
How is the Family Blessed with a Granddaughter?

Reflection Activity

1. In your role as a granddaughter, how have you been a blessing to your family? (In relation to your grandparents)

___
___
___
___
___

2. What are some things you can do to improve in your role as a granddaughter?

___
___
___
___
___

3. What do you need God to help you do?

___
___
___

F^1 = FAMILY: God Blesses The Family
How is the Family Blessed with a Grandson?

In light of the fact that I don't have a grandson yet, I have asked my mother to share her input with this section of the book because she has grandsons.

Many people have their own perspective of how they consider a grandson to be a blessing, however, I will share with you from her perspective.

She has shared that she believes a grandson should be communicative, stand out from most, be extremely friendly to relatives and friends, be willing to "give his shirt off of his back," (figuratively speaking), be helpful when needed, and most of all, he is forgiving and will always show love to all.

F^1 = FAMILY: God Blesses The Family
How is the Family Blessed with a Grandson?

Reflection Activity

1. In your role as a grandson, how have you been a blessing to your family? (In relation to your grandparents)

_____
_____
_____
_____
_____

2. What are some things you can do to improve in your role as a grandson?

_____
_____
_____
_____
_____

3. What do you need God to help you do?

_____
_____
_____

F^1 = FAMILY: God Blesses The Family
How is the Family Blessed with Grandchildren?

The Bible tells us in (Proverbs 17:6a) that "Grandchildren are the crowning glory of the aged."

According to www.bibleref.com "Family life is blessed when children cause their parents and grandparents to rejoice. Grandchildren can make their grandparents feel intense, selfless pride. Furthermore, children should be proud of their parents."

Grandchildren are a blessing to the family by the way they live and how they treat their parents and grandparents. Literally and figuratively, as I examine this verse, I visualize a crown on the grandparent's head. A crown is something you place on someone's head who is being recognized or honored as achieving some type of title.

I believe the title of "grandparent" is a special title that should be worn as a crown with humility, dignity, honor, and authority! The crown can be seen by everyone and should bring some type of praise to those who wear it because those who see it know that it is a symbol of accomplishment. When we look at the lives of our grandchildren, we would like to see that the teachings and examples we laid in the foundation of their parent's lives will cause them to have a solid life filled with the grace and blessings of God.

F^1 = FAMILY: God Blesses The Family
How is the Family Blessed with Grandchildren?

Speaking of crowns, in (1 Chronicles 20:2a) KJV, we are told: "David took the crown of their king from off his head, and found it to weigh a talent of gold, and there were precious stones in it; and it was set upon David's head..."

According to www.gotquestions.org , a talent in the Hebrew weighs about seventy-five (75) pounds. I was reminded of putting on a helmet as I rode on the back of my husband's Can-Am and my neck began to tire from the weight of it which could only have been about five pounds.

Imagine wearing the king's crown! It also had precious stones in it as well. As I continue to envision this crown in a literal and figurative sense, gold is something that holds value and precious stones are considered to be rare. Our grandchildren should bring value to the family and be viewed as a rare and precious blessing from God.

F^2 = FAITH: God Blesses Our Faith
How are We Blessed in Our Faith?

We've probably heard the Bible verse in (Hebrews 11:1) which states that faith is the substance of things hoped for and the evidence of things not seen. Most of us can quote it without looking it up in the Bible, but what does it REALLY mean? For me personally, I believe that faith is made up of the things I hope for and believe they will happen regardless of what I see. In other words, we walk by faith and not by sight, which is another familiar verse in (2 Corinthians 5:7).

How do we walk by faith and not by sight? Let me give you a real-life example. In May 2024, my sister and I had been invited to my cousin's high school graduation. The weather forecast projected that it was a 100% chance of rain and flash flooding up until about 1:00 p.m. The graduation was scheduled for 10:00 a.m. I could have easily allowed the forecast to deter me from attending the graduation but as I have always told my husband: "I believe in the God who can calm the raging seas," so I know he can stop the rain and flash floods with just a wave of His hand, or a word spoken from Heaven. So, as I drove to the graduation, it rained all the way there but when I arrived in the parking lot of the Civic Center, the rain had completely stopped, and it did not rain anymore that day. We were blessed to enjoy graduation as well as a family fellowship at my cousin's house without a raincoat or umbrella.

F^2 = FAITH: God Blesses Our Faith
How are We Blessed in Our Faith?

Faith Brings Salvation: Salvation is defined as the deliverance from the slavery of sin or some other distress by the intervention of God.

The Bible informs us that all we have to do is "confess" and "believe" in order to be saved. In (Romans 10:9-10 KJV), we are told: {"9 That if thou shalt confess with thy mouth the Lord Jesus, and shalt believe in thine heart that God hath raised him from the dead, thou shalt be saved. 10 For with the heart man believeth unto righteousness; and with the mouth confession is made unto salvation."}

Attaining Salvation is not complicated. We often make it complicated by trying to earn our way to God, but it is clearly stated in (Ephesians 2:8-9), that we are saved by God's grace and faith in Jesus Christ, and we can't take credit for it nor is Salvation a reward for the "good" things we have done.
It is a gift from God.

Now that we have discussed what Faith is and how to be saved, some might ask: "How do I increase my faith?" We will find the answer in (Romans 10:17). Faith comes from hearing the Good News about Jesus Christ, but we must not be "hearers" only but also "doers" of God's Word. (James 1:22)

F^2 = FAITH: God Blesses Our Faith
How are We Blessed in Our Faith?

Faith Brings Forgiveness and Justification:

Forgiveness is defined as a pardon or acquittal of sins; Justification is defined as the process of being justified or being made right with God.

Once we place our faith in Jesus Christ, we are forgiven and we must live a life pleasing to Him but often times we sin and fall short of His glory (Romans 3:23-24) and find ourselves in need of forgiveness and are justified freely by His grace through the redemption that is in Christ Jesus. We are told in (1 John 1:9), that if we confess our sins, He is faithful and just and will forgive us and cleanse us from all unrighteousness.

The suffix "tion" means the process of, so in the word Justification, we find the meaning as the process of being justified by God. This is a process and does not happen instantly. We are made right with God by what Jesus Christ did for us on Calvary. The New Living Translation puts it plainly: "He was handed over to die because of our sins, and He was raised to life to make us right with God." (Romans 4:25)

📖 Additional Bible Verses 📖
{(Galatians 2:16), (Galatians 3:24), (Philippians 3:8-9)}

F^2 = FAITH: God Blesses Our Faith
How are We Blessed in Our Faith?

Faith Brings Healing: To heal means to mend, cure, make whole; return to the original state of health.

The accounts of healing in the Bible are so numerous, it would be impossible to contain or discuss them all in this context, however we will focus on a few people who were healed as a result of their faith.

In (Matthew 8:1-4), Jesus heals a man of leprosy. This was definitely a "faith act" because during the Bible times, people who had leprosy were not allowed to be among people without leprosy. They were "banished from their homes and the city." They could only show themselves to the priest who would confirm they had been healed. However, this man's faith was so great that he risked being seen among others without leprosy and made his way to approach Jesus among a crowd of people. He knew that if Jesus was "willing," He could heal him. Jesus was indeed willing, and He reached out His hand to touch him and the man was healed. We may not have an "incurable" disease, but we have all been infected with the disease of "sin."

Won't you allow Jesus to touch and heal you today?

F² = FAITH: God Blesses Our Faith
How are We Blessed in Our Faith?

Faith Brings Healing: *To heal means to mend, cure, make whole; return to the original state of health.*

The Faith of a Roman Officer: (Matthew 8:5-10, 13)

Have you ever done anything that would cause Jesus to "marvel" over you? In other words, to be amazed by you or to wonder or admire you! There was a Roman Officer (also known as: Centurion-the captain of one hundred men) who had so much faith in Jesus, he believed Jesus could heal his servant just by speaking the Word because he felt unworthy of Jesus's presence at his home. When Jesus heard it, he marveled at the man's great faith as to compare it to all of Israel. The man's faith was rewarded with the healing of his servant and Jesus told him to go home and that what he believed for had happened within the same hour of the conversation. Glory to God for a renowned faith. This man could have allowed time, distance, pride, and/or prejudice to become an obstacle for him approaching and believing in Jesus. What is hindering you from coming to Jesus TODAY?

F² = FAITH: God Blesses Our Faith
How are We Blessed in Our Faith?

Jesus Heals the Woman with an Issue of Blood

In (Mark 5:25-34), we are told that as Jesus and His disciples were in route to the leader of the synagogue's house (aka: Jairus) He was detained by a woman who had an issue of blood for twelve (12) years. She was considered as being "unclean" and should not have been mingling with others. She defied the norm and pressed her way through the crowd and had so much faith in Jesus that she said within herself, that if she could only touch the hem of His garment, she knew she would be made whole. When Jesus realized He had been touched in a special way, (after all, the crowd was pressing their way to see Him) the healing virtue flowed out of Him, and the woman was made whole instantly. Jesus then turned around and asked who had touched Him and the woman fell at His feet and admitted it was her who touched Him and He told her that *her faith had healed her* and to go in peace and to be whole of her plague. What is plaguing you today? Will you give it to Jesus and be made whole?

F^2 = FAITH: God Blesses Our Faith
How are We Blessed in Our Faith?

Jesus Heals Blind Bartimaeus

In (Mark 10:46-52), a large crowd was following Jesus and among them was a blind man named Bartimaeus. He had heard Jesus was nearby, so he began to cry out: "Jesus, thou son of David, have mercy on me." Many tried to make him hold his peace, but he cried out even the more. Jesus heard him and stood still and called for him to come and he threw off his garment and came to Jesus. Jesus asked him what he wanted Him to do for him and he told Jesus that he wanted to receive his sight. Jesus told him his faith had healed him and he received his sight immediately and followed Jesus down the road.

The removal of the garment represented leaving the old life to seek after a life with Jesus. Will you leave your old life of sin to seek after a new life with Jesus? God is pleased and He rewards those who have faith in Him and diligently seek Him. (Hebrews 11:6)

F² = FAITH: God Blesses Our Faith
How are We Blessed in Our Faith?

Will You Be the One to Come Back?

In (Luke 17:11-19), Jesus healed ten (10) people with leprosy. Their determination and faith are commendable because they were an isolated group in their community who had been expelled from the common people. They had faith that Jesus could heal them by crying out and displayed their faith even more when Jesus told them to show themselves to the priest even before He healed them. They were healed as they were in route to the priest. Most people would probably focus on the ten people with leprosy as a whole, who were healed, in comparison to **the one** who came back to worship and praise God for his healing. He was the **"one"** who recognized that he had been healed on the way to see the priest and decided to turn around to **loudly tell Jesus thanks!** He was also a Samaritan (who was despised by the Jews as half breeds) and was the least likely to praise God. (John 4:9) Often times we forget to praise God for His blessings. We must seek God intentionally for our needs and praise Him for what He has already done!

F² = FAITH: God Blesses Our Faith
How are We Blessed in Our Faith?

Our Faith in God Draws Others to Christ

(Acts 2:37-41)

As a student of the Word, *(which is what I call myself because I am always learning)*, I must know and believe what I am learning so that I can begin teaching. Peter believed in what he was preaching so much so that it impacted the hearts of three thousand (3,000) believers being added to the church. Peter's preaching was filled with the Spirit of God, which convicted the people's hearts to turn (repent) from their sinful lives and live for Jesus. Peter told them to repent, be baptized, and be filled with the Holy Ghost. Faith in God and what His Son Jesus did for us is what saves us, **not Baptism**. "Baptism only identifies us with Christ and the community of believers." The verse in (Mark 16:16 KJV) reads: "He that believeth and is baptized shall be saved; but he that believeth not shall be damned." It does NOT say "he who baptizes not, shall be damned."

F² = FAITH: God Blesses Our Faith
How are We Blessed in Our Faith?

Faith Brings Encouragement

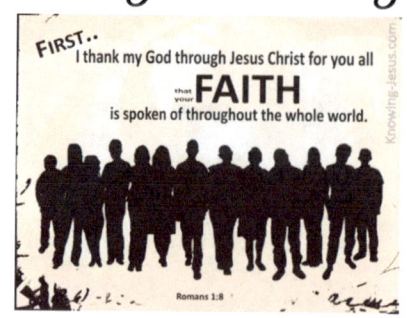

In (Romans 1:8-12), Paul begins by encouraging the believers in their faith by informing them that their faith had become world renowned. As believers, it is our responsibility to encourage and pray for other believers and for those who do not yet have a relationship with Jesus Christ.

Paul was a prime example of a prayer warrior for other believers. At times, we become discouraged in our faith walk and we need to be encouraged by someone else and it is our genuine faith in God that encourages other believers. I admire how Paul expressed himself in (Romans 1:12) by saying: "When we get together, I want to encourage you in your faith, but I also want to be encouraged by yours." When you get together with other believers, do you encourage them in their faith? Do they in return, encourage you in your faith? If not, why not? If so, how has it enabled you to continue to persevere in your walk with God regardless of the challenges?

Read {(1 Thessalonians 1:1-10) and (1 Thessalonians 3:1-8).}

F² = FAITH: God Blesses Our Faith
How are We Blessed in Our Faith?

Faith Brings Unity

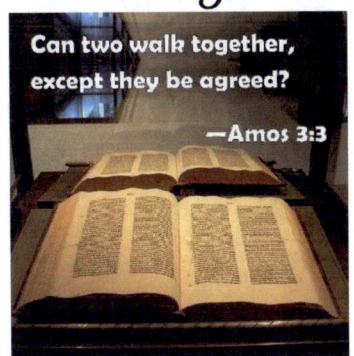

http://www.photos-public-domain.com/

As I was preparing to study the verses about faith bringing unity, the Holy Spirit dropped this verse in my spirit. How can two people walk together except they agree on the direction? I believe this verse is about unity. As believers of Jesus Christ, (who is the Head of the Body of Christ), **we are ONE**. Unity does not happen overnight, it takes work.

This work *"will continue until we all come to such unity in our faith and knowledge of God's Son that we will be mature in the Lord, measuring up to the full and complete standard of Christ."*

Differences among people can cause division but we must remember to focus on what unites us. We are **one body, serving one Lord, having one faith, one baptism and serving the one true and living God!** Read {(Ephesians 4:1-13), (1 Corinthians 12:12-13).}

Even though we have differing gifts, we must use those gifts to help build up, strengthen, and encourage the church. Read the verses below for more on Spiritual Gifts.
{(Romans 12:6-8), (1 Corinthians 12:4-11, 28), and (Ephesians 4:11).}

F^2 = FAITH: God Blesses Our Faith
How are We Blessed in Our Faith?

Faith Brings Joy and Peace

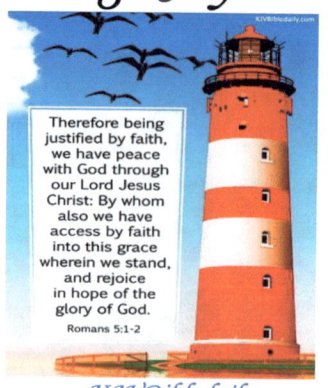

Paul is telling us in (Romans 5:1-2), that because we are justified by faith in Jesus Christ, we have **peace** with God. That means we are no longer enemies and we are in right standing with God and we have been reconciled with God. When we were in this world and living as the world, we were enemies to God. (James 4:4) Do you remember what it felt like to be at odds with someone and the issue remained unresolved? The burdensome feelings of anger and guilt knowing you should do something to bring about the **peace** and **joy** of reconciliation between you and the offended party. I always say it is so much easier to be **joyful** than angry. It takes too much energy to remain angry and to be at odds with people. Our faith in Jesus Christ resulted in our reconciliation and **peace** with God, which ultimately brings us **joy**! Because of our faith, we have access to God's grace (His unmerited favor) and the hope of God's glory also brings us JOY!!!

F² = FAITH: God Blesses Our Faith
How are We Blessed in Our Faith?

Faith Fulfills the Promise of the Holy Spirit

> Did you receive the Spirit by the works of the law, or by hearing of faith? Are you so foolish? Having begun in the Spirit, are you now completed in the flesh?
> Galatians 3:2-3
> talktotheword.com

(Galatians 3:2-3)

Just as we are saved by grace and not by our works, we receive the Holy Spirit by our faith in Jesus Christ, and not by following the Law. References: (Galatians 3:14) and (Ephesians 2:8-9).

> **THE HOLY SPIRIT IS GOD'S GUARANTEE**
> When you believed in Christ, God identified you as His own by giving you the Holy Spirit, whom He promised long ago. The Spirit is God's guarantee that He will give us the inheritance He promised and that He has purchased us to be His own people. He did this so we would praise and glorify Him.
> Ephesians 1:13-14

https://www.tumblr.com/wiirocku/148743812591/ephesians-113-14-nlt-and-now-you-gentiles

It is hard for some people to believe that we receive the Holy Spirit when we first believed, however the Holy Spirit is God's guarantee that we will receive everything that He has promised. Some people may even imply that this verse in (Luke 11:13) states that we have to ask for the Holy Spirit. I believe this verse is a reminder to persist in prayer by the power of the Holy Spirit which is God's greatest gift to the believer. Reference: (Ephesians 1:13-14).

F^2 = FAITH: God Blesses Our Faith
How are We Blessed in Our Faith?

Faith Provides Weapons to Fight the Enemy

FreeBibleimages.com

The world we live in is full of warfare. Not just in a military sense, but in a spiritual sense. Demons are real and the only way to fight them is with spiritual weapons because we don't fight against flesh and blood. Many times, we have "fights" with people, it is because the spirit in them is fighting against the spirit in us. This is called spiritual warfare. (Galatians 5:16-17)

In (Ephesians 6:11-18), Paul encourages the believers to put on the whole armor of God so we will be able to stand against the wiles of the devil. We are specifically told that "In addition to all of these (weapons), to hold up the shield of faith to stop the fiery arrows of the devil." (Ephesians 6:16) Our faith in God's power and His Word, helps us to dispel all the lies of the devil and overcome any adversity he throws our way. "For every child of God defeats this evil world and we achieve this victory through our faith. And who can win this battle against this world? Only those who believe that Jesus is the Son of God." (1 John 5:4-5)

F^2 = FAITH: God Blesses Our Faith
How are We Blessed in Our Faith?

Faith Helps us Believe the So-Called "Impossible"

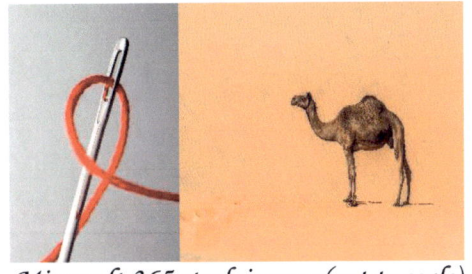

Microsoft 365 stock images (not to scale)

Can you imagine a camel going through the eye of a needle? Most of us have seen a needle in person and perhaps a camel on television or at the zoo. Literally speaking, could this happen? The answer would be "NO"! So, then what did Jesus mean when He told His disciples that a rich man could not enter into the Kingdom of God, and that it was easier for a camel to go through the eye of a needle, than for a rich man to enter into the Kingdom of God? Jesus used a form of exaggeration for the disciples to realize that with man, this would not be possible, but with God, all things are possible. In other words, if a rich person is relying on his riches to get into heaven, it would be impossible. There are many rich people who love the Lord and will go to heaven. However, if you think because you are rich, and that it is an automatic entrance into heaven, you are sadly mistaken. The moral of the story in (Matthew 19:16-26) is that following the Law does not save us and we can't love our possessions more than God.

F^2 = FAITH: God Blesses Our Faith
How are We Blessed in Our Faith?

Our Faith Helps us to Please God

Hebrews 11:6
And without Faith it is impossible to please God, because anyone who comes to Him must Believe that He exists and that He rewards those who earnestly Seek Him.

https://www.pinterest.com/pin/33636328440825179/

As you read about the definition of faith and the great examples of faith in (Hebrews 11:1-40), you will find some amazing people who were humans just like us but were able to do some amazing things because they had great faith in God to do what seemed foolish and somewhat impossible from a human's mindset. Were they perfect in their walk with God? No, however we are striving for perfection.

Be encouraged in your faith as you read about Enoch who was taken up to heaven without dying, Noah who built an ark to save his family from the flood when there was no rain, and Sarah who became pregnant at 90 years old, etc.

F^2 = FAITH: God Blesses Our Faith
How are We Blessed in Our Faith?

Faith Produces Good Works

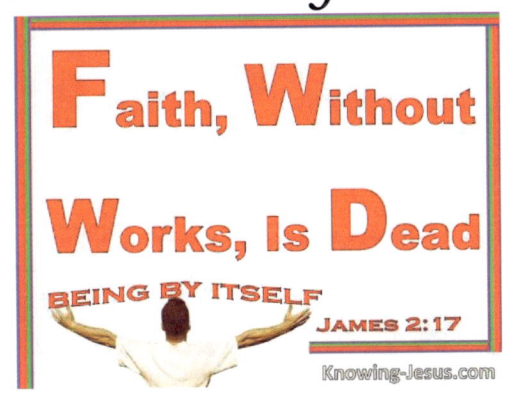

It is easy to say we have faith, but when our faith requires us to take some action, we find ourselves being a little reluctant.

Faith without action can't save anyone. What if we see a brother or sister in need and we pass them by without another thought? Most of us have done it because we have more than likely experienced some form of swindle from beggars who aren't really in need. If the Holy Spirit prompts us to meet a need, it is our Christian duty to do so. James reminds us that faith without works is dead in the verse above.

Abraham put his faith into action when he was willing to sacrifice his only son Isaac. (Genesis 22:1-19) Rahab risked her life to assist the spies, which resulted in the deliverance of her family from destruction. (Joshua 2:1-24) It took faith in action for Abram to obey God by leaving his country and family to go to another land in which he did not know where he was going and how he was going to live. (Genesis 12:1-9)

F² = FAITH: God Blesses Our Faith
How are We Blessed in Our Faith?

Faith Produces Good Works (Part 2)

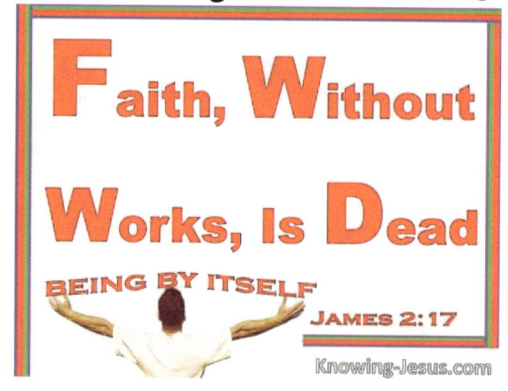

It was faith in action when Moses's mother hid him in a basket and put him in the river because she believed that he would be safe from genocide ordered by the king. (Exodus 2:1-10) It was faith in action when Naomi and Ruth returned back to their land in hopes that God would provide for them during the famine. (Ruth 1:6-18) It was faith in action when Moses held up the rod to part the Red Sea to allow the children of Israel to march across the Red Sea on dry land while trusting God to deliver them from Egypt. (Exodus 14:15-16) It was faith in action when the people of Israel marched around Jericho seven days to see the walls come tumbling down as an example of God's power. (Joshua 6:1-21) How many more examples do I need to list? It would take too long for me to list all the accounts in the Bible where faith was in action. Faith is an action word! **If our faith does not compel us to action, it is dead faith and it is useless!**

F^2 = FAITH: God Blesses Our Faith
How are We Blessed in Our Faith?

Faith Produces Good Works (Part 3)

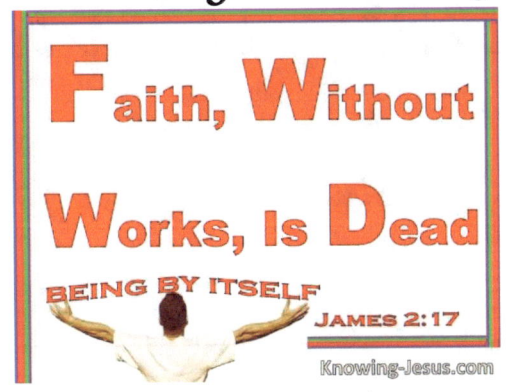

Now, let's take a look at your life. It was faith in action when you laid down last night to close your eyes to go to sleep while believing that God would sustain your breathing and heartbeat and would touch you with His finger of love to awaken you according to His will. It takes faith in action for you to drive a car and trust God to sustain its workmanship. It takes faith in action for you to sit on a pew in church and believe that God will allow it to hold you up. It takes faith in action to get on a plane and believe God will allow it to ascend into the clouds and return to the ground. It takes faith in action to pay your tithes and give to others in need while trusting God to meet your needs. It takes faith in action when you plant seeds in the ground and water them only to trust God for the crop. And yes, God is in control of your garden. It is not you who makes it grow.
{Additional Scripture References: (Malachi 3:10), (Philippians 4:19).}

F^2 = FAITH: God Blesses Our Faith
How are We Blessed in Our Faith?

Reflection Activity

1. In your role as a Christian, how have you been blessed by your faith?

_____
_____
_____
_____

2. What are some things you can do to increase your faith?

_____
_____
_____
_____
_____

3. What do you need God to help you do in relation to your faith?

_____
_____
_____

F³ = Friends: God Blesses Our Friendships
How are We Blessed in Our Friendships?

Friends are Friendly

As I give serious and careful thought to the initiation and culmination of my friendships, I would hope that I could conclude that I have been found to be "friendly" in my relationships with others. I have met a lot of people over the course of the sixty-one years (61) I have been in this world thus far (2024). I have discovered that "associates" are not necessarily "friends." Everyone you meet will not be connected to you as a friend. I believe a friend is one who cares about you and understands you just as you are without trying to change you. A friend who is "friendly" shows joy, kindness and genuine concern for your overall well-being and has things in common with you. This type of friend strives to enhance your life not to hinder growth in your life. In other words, you should become a better person and friend as you engage with this kind of friendship.

F^3 = Friends: God Blesses Our Friendships
How are We Blessed in Our Friendships?

Faithful Friends Persevere

In (Mark 2:1-12), Jesus was teaching the Word of God in a house where He was visiting and there were so many people, there was no room left inside or outside the house. In the meantime, there were four (4) friends who were determined to get their friend (who was sick of the palsy) to Jesus. They climbed up to the roof and tore it open and lowered their friend down into the house where Jesus was. Jesus was aware that it took great faith to do this and He told the sick man that his sins were forgiven and He was accused of blasphemy because only God could forgive sins. Jesus is the Son of God and can forgive sins (Mark 2:10) and not only that, but He also told the man to get up from his mat, pick it up and go home. He did as he was told, was healed, and forgiven and they were all amazed and began to glorify God! Do your friends see your needs and go above and beyond to meet them or do they make excuses or allow things to hinder them? A friend who is a blessing will do whatever they can to help you or direct you to the One who can!

F³ = Friends: God Blesses Our Friendships
How are We Blessed in Our Friendships?

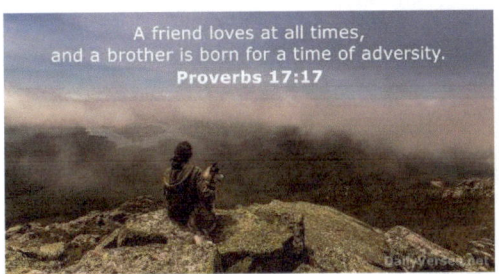

True Friends are Loyal

This is one of my favorite Bible verses. It is a reminder that friends should be loyal to each other. As friends, we don't have to condone each other's wrongdoing, however we still have to love one another. Besides, we have all probably heard the expression of a "fair-weather" friend. This friend only relates to you when there is "no rain" or any type of problems or adversities in your life or theirs. We live in this world and we will always face tribulations. (John 16:33)

We have also been told in (1 Peter 4:8) that LOVE covers a multitude of sins. This means that our love for others is GREATER than their failures and we should be willing to forgive and to love them unconditionally. Does this mean that we should never confront the wrong in our relationships? Absolutely not! The Word tells us in (Proverbs 27:6, 9) the wounds from a sincere friend are better than many kisses from an enemy. This verse implies that it is better to listen to unpleasant (helpful) advice from a friend than to listen to lies whispered in his ear by the enemy. The heartfelt counsel of a friend is like sweet perfume.

F³ = Friends: God Blesses Our Friendships
How are We Blessed in Our Friendships?

True Friends will Sharpen You

As I think on the process of iron sharpening, I envision two pieces of iron engaging with each other in a rubbing or shaping fashion. As this process continues, the two pieces of iron become sharper. As two friends engage with each other, they should both become sharper and more effective.

The conversations you have should build you up and not tear you down. As friends reflect on life, they should accentuate the positives and pray about the negatives. When friends speak about each other, it should be in a manner to build them up and not tear them down and if there is a negative or discouraging situation in the relationship, it should be taken to the Lord in prayer not given to the street committee so to speak. Instead of saying: "Let me tell you about what I heard..." Begin by saying: "Let us pray about..."!

A troublemaker plants seeds of strife; gossip separates the best of friends." (Proverbs 16:28)

F³ = Friends: God Blesses Our Friendships
How are We Blessed in Our Friendships?

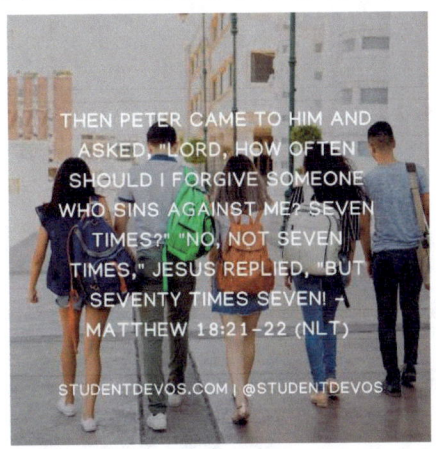

True Friends are Forgiving

In this Bible verse, according to the *New Living Translation* commentary, Rabbis had been teaching that people only had to forgive each other three (3) times. Presuming that Peter, desiring to be somewhat gracious, used the number seven (7) (as it is the number of completion in the Bible,) as he approached Jesus to ask about the number of times he should forgive someone who sins against him. Jesus replied: "No, not seven times, but seventy times seven." Mathematically speaking this would amount to a total of four hundred ninety times (70 x 7=490) but Jesus did not mean this in a literal or mathematical sense, but He meant that we **should not keep track** of how many times we forgive. Could you imagine trying to keep track of the number of times someone sinned against you or vice versa? In forgiving others, we will quickly discover that it is more for our benefit and not just theirs. Please read (Matthew 6:14-15) for more information on forgiveness!

F³ = Friends: God Blesses Our Friendships
How are We Blessed in Our Friendships?

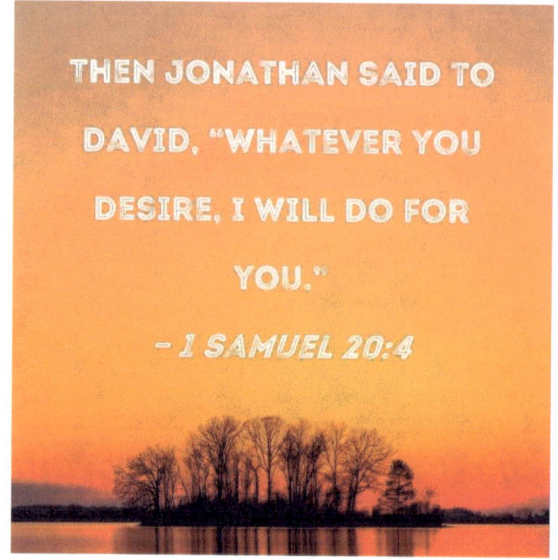

True Friends are Helpful

Many would find it hard to help a friend especially if it meant you had to defy your own father. How could you? You may ask! When we stand for righteousness, it sometimes means you have to go against your family members. (Luke 12:52-53)

David and Jonathan were friends who were loyal to each other but were faced with the dilemma that Jonathan's father (the king Saul) was jealous of David and wanted to kill him. However, in light of Jonathan's faithfulness to his friendship with David, he vowed to help him. True friends are helpful even when they have to face adverse reactions from close family members as well as others.

Please take some time to read (1 Samuel 20:1-42) for the details of this story.

F³ = Friends: God Blesses Our Friendships
How are We Blessed in Our Friendships?

> If your gift is to encourage others, be encouraging. If it is giving, give generously. If God has given you leadership ability, take the responsibility seriously. And if you have a gift for showing kindness to others, do it gladly.
> Romans 12:8 NLT

https://www.tumblr.com/wiirocku/16413883

Friends Encourage One Another

Paul is one of the most encouraging people in the Bible that I have studied about. One of his spiritual gifts is exhortation which is just another word for being encouraging by offering words of comfort and consolation. The words of the godly encourage many, therefore, our words should be used to encourage one another. (Proverbs 10:21a) Everything we say should be good and helpful so that our words will be an encouragement to those who hear them. (Ephesians 4:29)

Encouraging words give us strength to persevere in our faith. {(Daniel 10:19), (1 Thessalonians 2:12; 3:2-3, 7-8; 5:14), (Acts 11:23; 13:15; 14:22; 16:40)}

If your friends are not encouraging you, find encouragement in the Word of God (Romans 15:4-5) and in the power of your prayers. (James 5:16b)

F³ = Friends: God Blesses Our Friendships
How are We Blessed in Our Friendships?

Freepik.com

Friends Strive for Reconciliation

In (Philippians 4:2-3), Paul states: "Now I appeal to Euodia and Syntyche. Please, because you belong to the Lord, settle your disagreement. And I ask you, my true partner, to help these two women, for they worked hard with me in telling others the Good News. They worked along with Clement and the rest of my co-workers, whose names are written in the Book of Life."

Paul intervenes in the broken relationship between Euodia and Syntyche. The text does not discuss the details of how this relationship became broken, however, Paul, being a peacemaker, felt the need for these two women to be reconciled because he didn't want the spreading of the Good News to be hindered by a disagreement. In our mutual friendships with one another, we may have disagreements but we will find it is important not to take sides but only to encourage the friends to talk it out and come to an agreement. Paul wanted these two women to be of the same mind in relation to Christ. Whatever our disagreements, it cannot take priority over the importance of a unified purpose in spreading the Good News. Put aside your differences and seek for peace, unity, and reconciliation in your friendships.

F³ = Friends: God Blesses Our Friendships
How are We Blessed in Our Friendships?

As I close this chapter of the book, I would like to summarize how my friends have been a blessing in my life. As I have experienced multiple facets of life in which friendships are originated, (i.e., childhood, middle school, high school, college, workplace, Christianity, etc.), I will attempt to summarize in an effective manner. First of all, allow me to reiterate that everyone you meet will not be considered a "friend" but an acquaintance or associate. I believe a friend makes a positive difference in your life, is supportive and makes contact with you periodically.

I have one childhood friend who comes to mind and we lived across the street from each other. She has impacted my life with her texts, calls, prayers, and lunch dates.

My friend from high school has impacted my life by texting me her work schedule so we can have lunch, inviting me to Vacation Bible School at her church and by praying for me and my family.

I met several people as I was in college but only about four of them are considered friends and have been a blessing in my life with their texts to check on me, prayers, prayer line invitations, meeting me when I was in town just to say hello, sending me encouraging text messages, lunch dates, and virtual Bible Study invitations.

F³ = Friends: God Blesses Our Friendships
How are We Blessed in Our Friendships?

I currently have four friends in heaven. 😇 They were a blessing as well by texting, calling, praying for me, sharing the Word, sending text updates concerning their health, and one of them even recommended me for the Payroll Assistant position at my college after graduation and she even allowed me to live with her for 14 months until I saved up for a car and an apartment before marriage.

As I have met many people over the years, some of which are friends and some are associates and/or acquaintances, there are a few more honorable mentions which consist of five women who readily comes to mind as friends and one of them blesses me with a "Good Morning" text very frequently and that lets me know she is thinking about me and we have often prayed together.

Another one of my friends has been a blessing to me because she sends me inspiring friendship cards in the mail out of the blue, has assisted me with the ministries at the church (and never complains), and she takes walks with me at the park and at the mall as we sharpen iron and pray, and she has showered me with heartfelt gifts on some Birthdays, Mother's Days, and Christmases, even though she has a great deal of responsibilities.

F^3 = Friends: God Blesses Our Friendships
How are We Blessed in Our Friendships?

I have another friend who I met in my former church over 20 years ago and she blesses me by helping with major cleaning and outreach projects. She also encourages me with inspiring texts and prayers.

Another friend who comes to mind has to travel for work and she would send me texts to let me know she was coming through town and I would offer lunch and hospitality as we would sharpen iron on the sunporch during which time, she surprised me with a bouquet of fresh flowers and she would send me texts to check on me and she also inspires me by the way she has persevered through many challenges in her own relationships.

I also have a pastor friend who invited me to her church to teach Bible Study using the Lord's Obedience book and she sends encouraging scripture based texts occasionally. She also inspired me as she would post her sermons live on Facebook.

In addition, I have friends from the workplace who have blessed my life by being team players on our team when I was Team Leader, monitoring my students when I needed a restroom break, completing special cleaning or repair requests, sharing the workload and ideas during collaboration, seeking my hand and faith for prayer requests, reading and/or purchasing my published books, calling to check on me and assisting with my retirement process, purchased gifts for holidays and my retirement, etc.

F^3 = Friends: God Blesses Our Friendships
How are We Blessed in Our Friendships?

*Another friend has blessed me with her **spontaneous texts** to inquire if I was busy so we could plan our **talks and walks** at the track, and we definitely share the Word and prayers with each other and she surprised me with a **birthday lunch in April 2024**. She and her husband also surprised me by **attending our church** one Sunday.*

*Another friend has blessed me with **encouraging words** and text messages in the workplace and has sent me **virtual Bible Study invitations** from her family members who were doing Bible Study on the phone during Covid 19 and she **inspired me** by telling me that if she ever became principal, she would hire me as one of her teachers. She would often say that my interactions with her three girls provided the practice I needed to become a grandmama.*

*I have another friend who probably views me as a mentor more than a friend, because she is young enough to be my daughter, and I have shared some teaching and relationship experiences with her, however, she blesses me with her **random texts and pictures** to keep me up to date with her trips with her new husband or her latest career endeavors.*

F³ = Friends: God Blesses Our Friendships
How are We Blessed in Our Friendships?

Last, but not least, I must mention that I have three friends who I literally call my "sister-neighbor-friends" because they are my sisters-in-Christ, my neighbors, and my friends.

The first one blesses me with her **sweet humble spirit** as we talk on the phone, cry, and pray together. We have also had visits at the fence where we would **talk, hug and almost cry** and we have **shared our homes and food** from her garden and Salt Lick. She and her husband often **look out for us** and the property when we're out of town and will often allow our guests to **park** on their vacant property when we have large gatherings.

The second one blessed me with **impromptu visits to pick up or drop off treats** and was instrumental in arranging my first **book signing** for the Obedience book and she was also a fantastic Language Arts teacher to my children.

The third one blessed me with **walks in the neighborhood** and **shared produce from her garden**. Please don't take offense if I didn't make reference to you as a friend. I am grateful for everyone who has impacted my life, including the stranger.

F³ = Friends: God Blesses Our Friendships
How are We Blessed in Our Friendships?

Reflection Activity

1. In your role as a friend, how have you been a blessing to your friends?

_____
_____
_____
_____

2. What are some things you can do to improve in your role as a friend?

_____
_____
_____
_____

3. What do you need God to help you do in relation to your friends?

_____
_____
_____

.F⁴ = Fellowship: God Blesses Our Fellowships
How are We Blessed in Our Fellowships?

https://www.scripture-images.com/

Fellowship is defined as friendship, association, company, or partnership. It is befitting to mention that first and foremost, we are blessed in our fellowships because God invited us to have fellowship with His Son, Jesus Christ. In (Genesis 3:8-9), God called out to Adam and Eve because He wanted to spend time with them. He called out to them but they had sinned and disobeyed God and hid themselves (or so they thought).

It sort of reminds me of a parent calling out to a child who has been quiet for a while and the parental instincts urge them to call out to them to make sure they are not involved in any mischief. Adam and Eve "hid themselves" because after they sinned, they felt embarrassed and guilty and realized their nakedness and therefore clothed themselves with fig leaves. Isn't that how we behave? We become distant from God and try to hide from Him because our sinfulness has caused us to feel guilty and ashamed. God sees and knows all and He only wants to draw us back to Him and away from our sinfulness. (James 4:8)

F^4 = Fellowship: God Blesses Our Fellowships
How are We Blessed in Our Fellowships?

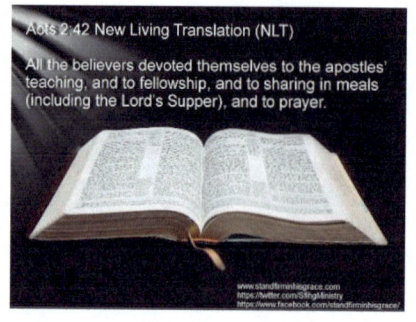

The writer Luke in the image verse above explains how believers were devoted in joining together in fellowship to partake of God's Word, Communion, other meals, and prayer. Speaking of fellowships, my husband's mother's side of the family had a wonderful fellowship by way of a family reunion. We had a well-planned, eventful weekend between July 12-14, 2024. Friday we met for registration, music, food, conversation, dancing and witnessing of selfless love and service for family. Saturday we met for a family memorial which included family history, singing, reflection of faith, and a banquet filled with beautiful people, outfits, delicious food, fun, conversations, laughter, dancing and making lasting memories. How relevant for my husband to share (Hebrews 10:24-25) as the scripture on Saturday, which reminds us to think of ways to motivate one another to acts of love and good works and not to forsake our meeting together especially since the day of Jesus's return is drawing near. Sunday, we gathered for worship, the Word of God, prayer, and showering of gifts to the youth for their academic accomplishments. We met a man there who blessed us with a watermelon because we did not have any cash in hand and he did not have the Cash App for us to pay him.

I was blessed to even share a few leftover prayer books for Moms from Mother's Day and Bible Verse cards with the family!

F^4 = Fellowship: God Blesses Our Fellowships
How are We Blessed in Our Fellowships?

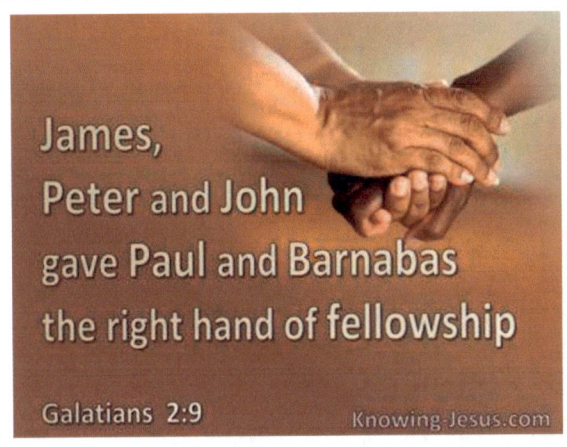

Paul continues to describe the blessings of fellowship when three disciples gave him and Barnabas the "right hand of fellowship" which signified their acceptance of them as fellow co-workers of spreading the Gospel and they also encouraged them to keep preaching to the Gentiles and they in return, encouraged them to continue their work with the Jews.

Those affiliated with the Baptist Church may have heard the phrase: "right hand of fellowship." I never knew there was an actual verse in the Bible that speaks about this tradition in the church until I began my study on fellowship. However, it is the church's way of accepting new believers or new members. Paul also tells us in (Philippians 1:5) that our fellowship with others in spreading the Gospel, makes us a valuable asset to the building of God's Kingdom and affords us the privilege of praying for other believers.

F⁴ = Fellowship: God Blesses Our Fellowships
How are We Blessed in Our Fellowships?

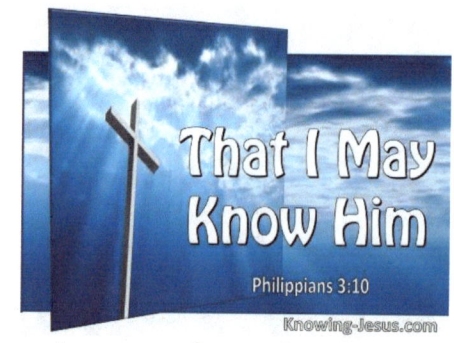

In (Philippians 3:10), Paul is letting us know that in our "fellowship of suffering," we become acquainted with Christ Jesus through suffering. You may ask how is this a blessing? The Word also tells us in (2 Timothy 2:12) that if we suffer with Christ, we will also reign with Him. Therefore, when we suffer, it helps us to relate to what Christ suffered when He was crucified on the cross. It is similar to when you experience hardships the same as a friend, then you begin to relate to that friend even more. "Or have you forgotten that when we were joined with Christ Jesus in baptism, we joined Him in His death? For we died and were buried with Christ by baptism. And just as Christ was raised from the dead by the glorious power of the Father, now we also may live new lives. Since we have been united with him in his death, we will also be raised to life as He was." (Romans 6:3-5)

In a nutshell, Paul is just letting us know that the same power that resurrected Jesus Christ will also resurrect believers in Jesus Christ, however, we cannot experience the power of the resurrection without the crucifixion. That is why Paul says he was "crucified with Christ," and like Paul, the life we live is through faith in Christ Jesus. (Galatians 2:20)

F^4 = Fellowship: God Blesses Our Fellowships
How are We Blessed in Our Fellowships?

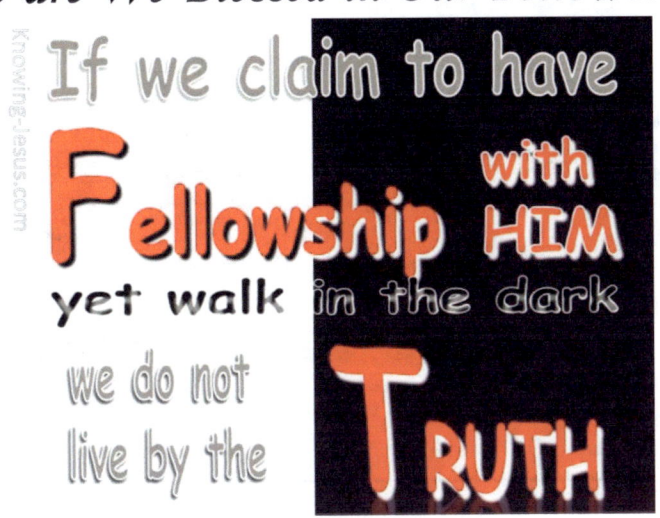

We are blessed in our fellowship with God, only if we walk in the light and not in darkness. (1 John 1:6-7) Light and darkness cannot co-exist. Light will overcome darkness every time. (John 1:5) If you are in a darkroom and a light from any source is illuminated, there is no longer darkness.

If we say we have fellowship with God but continue to walk in darkness, we do not live by the truth.

As Jesus explained why He had to die, He told the people to walk in the Light while they still could because He knew His time in person with them was coming to an end and they needed to become children of the Light. (John 12:35-36)

Jesus is the light of the world (John 8:12), and as His children, we have His light. We are told to let our light shine before men so they may see our good works and glorify our Father which is in Heaven. (Matthew 5:16)

F^4 = Fellowships: God Blesses Our Fellowships
How are We Blessed in Our Fellowships?

Reflection Activity

1. Discuss the last time you attended a fellowship:
(i.e., church, party, baby shower, wedding, etc.)

_____
_____
_____
_____

2. What are some things you enjoyed about the fellowship?

_____
_____
_____
_____

3. What do you think was the overall benefit of your attendance?

_____
_____

4. If you could have a "do-over", what would you change?

_____
_____

F^5 = Finances: God Blesses Our Finances
How are We Blessed in Our Finances?

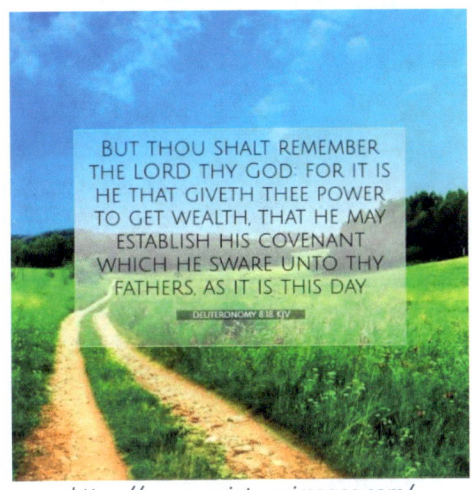

https://www.scripture-images.com/

This verse was a reminder to the children of Israel (and to us) not to forget that God gives us the power to get and steward our wealth. He also takes care of our needs (Philippians 4:19) and He provided for the Israelites as they wandered in the wilderness for forty (40) years. He provided them with food, water, protection, guidance, deliverance, and raiment that withstood the elements. When things are going well and we have plenty, it is easy to think we are doing it in our own power and ability. (Deuteronomy 8:1-20) But, the minute things are of the contrary, we want God's help but don't want to necessarily acknowledge that He gives us provisions and the power to become wealthy. Not everyone will be rich but God's wisdom teaches us how to take our gifts, talents and abilities and use them to generate an income. This is an indication of how blessed we are in our finances.

F^5 = Finances: God Blesses Our Finances
How are We Blessed in Our Finances?

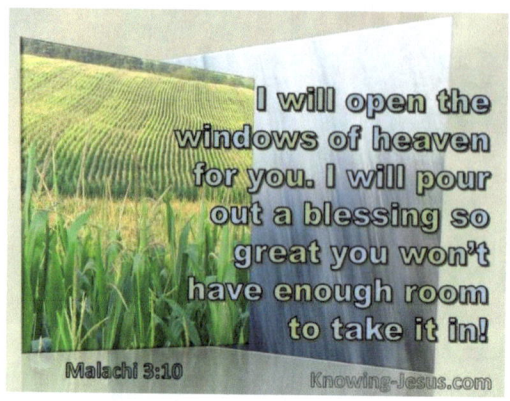

Since God gives us the ability to get wealth, should we not honor Him by paying our tithes? There are at least thirteen (13) verses in the Bible that use the word "tithe" and the word "tithes" is used in at least twenty-one (21) verses. These verses are located in the Old and New Testaments. Many people believe that we are not held accountable for paying our tithes in this modern society. The Word never fails and does not change just as the Lord never changes. He is the same yesterday, today, and forever. (Hebrews 13:8) The verse above is (Malachi 3:10b), however part A of this verse is the "conditional" part of this blessing. It states: "Bring all the tithes into the storehouse so there will be enough food in my temple, if you do says the Lord of Heaven's Army"... the word "if" is a "conditional" word, so that means we have to do something if we are expecting the other thing to happen. In this case, paying our tithes blesses our finances, however we don't pay tithes expecting something in return. We give to honor God, help others, and to bless our spiritual leaders. We have to watch our motives when giving. (1 Timothy 5:17-18)

F^5 = Finances: God Blesses Our Finances
How are We Blessed in Our Finances?

Speaking of motives for giving. As I was studying the Word about giving, I discovered a verse that stood out to me and I also discovered that I had made a note in the margins of my study Bible. The verse was from (Genesis 28:20-22). It is based on a vow that Jacob made to God after he visited him in a dream at Bethel and God promised him and his descendants land, and declared they would be as numerous as the dust of the earth, and that all families would be blessed by them, and promised him protection and to be with him until He had given him everything He had promised. After he awakened from the dream, he was convinced the Lord had visited that place. This is what he said: {"20 Then Jacob made this vow: If God will indeed be with me and protect me on this journey, and if he will provide me with food and clothing, 21 and if I return safely to my father's home, then the Lord will certainly be my God. 22 And this memorial pillar I have set up will become a place for worshiping God, and I will present to God a tenth of everything he gives me" (Genesis 28:20-22)}.

Notice the colored words: the if-then principle.

Some may view this vow as a "bargaining" tool but I believe Jacob was genuinely trying to commit to a relationship with God and knowing God had blessed him, he vowed to give God a "tenth" of **EVERYTHING!** *Sounds like tithing to me!*

F^5 = Finances: God Blesses Our Finances
How are We Blessed in Our Finances?

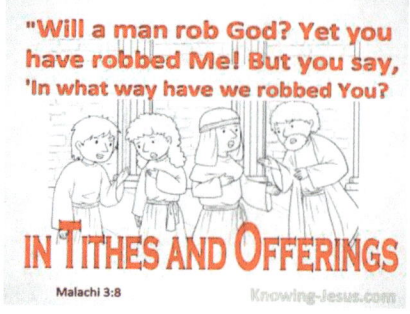

In Biblical times many paid **tithes** with fruit, (Leviticus 27:30) (Numbers 18:26), grains, vegetables, wine, olive oil, (Nehemiah 10:37; 13:15) animals, (Deuteronomy 12:6), honey, (2 Chronicles 31:5) spices, (Matthew 23:23) herbs, (Luke 11:42) etc., because it was their primary way to make a living in addition to people purchasing their crops. This Biblical form of **tithing** was necessary to provide food for the temple workers (i.e., priests, Levites).

Many believe the New Testament does not specifically address the principle of **tithing**, however, (Matthew 23:23) and (Luke 11:42) use the word "tithe," which is defined in the Greek (G586) as giving, paying or taking (without the mention of the word "tenth.") However, in (Hebrews 7:6, 8, 9) the word "tithes" is used to mean in the Greek (G1183 and G1181) as to give a **tenth**. Specifically, in (Malachi 3:10), and many other Old Testament verses, the word "tithes" is used to mean in Hebrew as a **tenth** or an accumulation of **tithes** (H4643 and H6237).

F^5 = Finances: God Blesses Our Finances
How are We Blessed in Our Finances?

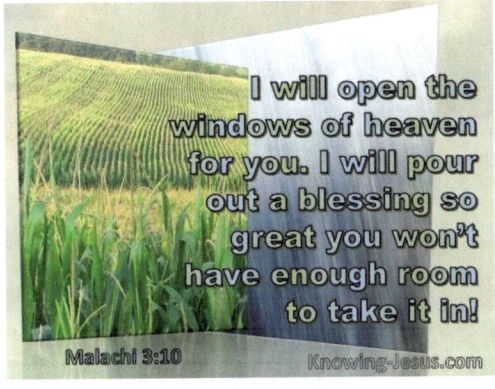

Today, we can be a blessing by paying our tithes which can help the pastor, minister or elder. {(1 Timothy 5:17-18), (Galatians 6:6), (Luke 10:7) and (1 Corinthians 9:4-10)} I have heard many people say they don't pay tithes because the people in charge of the money don't manage it correctly or they assume the leader is using the money for personal gain. In (Genesis 14:17-24), Abram (aka Abraham) gave a tenth of all the goods he recovered to the king of Salem (and the priest of God). According to the New Living Translation commentary, it was a pagan tradition to pay a tenth of one's earnings to the gods, so Abram was following the acceptable tradition. However, he refused to take any of the goods offered him from the king because he wanted people to know that God made him rich, not man. Traditionally from a Christian perspective, the tithe belongs to God. As we are making decisions about giving, we must remember that tithing does not excuse us from obeying God in other areas of our lives {(i.e., condemning others (Luke 18:12), showing justice, mercy, and faith (Matthew 23:23), taking care of widows (1 Timothy 5:3) and parents (Matthew 5:1-5).}

> We can give in many ways but what is most important is that we give according to how we are able, according to how we have purposed in our hearts, and to give willingly not reluctantly, not grudgingly, or under pressure or compulsion (being forced to do so or against what is in your conscience to give) because God loves a cheerful giver (2 Corinthians 9:7)

F^5 = Finances: God Blesses Our Finances
How are We Blessed in Our Finances?

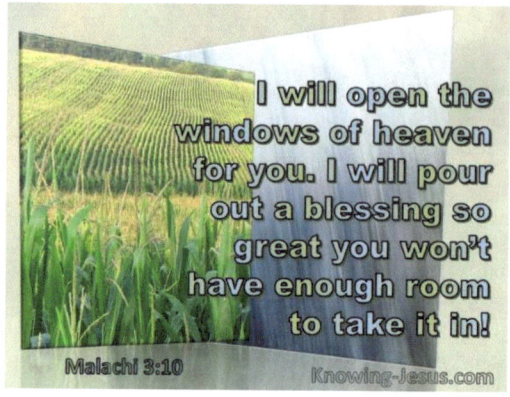

Today, it is my personal belief that we can still be blessed by paying our tithes and not view tithing as an Old Testament requirement. For example, a farmer can pay tithes from his crop if he is not selling anything. For example, if he has harvested 1,000 pounds of crops, he can give away 100 pounds to someone else or donate it to the church or mission food bank as payment of his tithes. If he is able to sell his crops, he can honor God with ten percent (10%) of his earnings.

It is also my personal belief that when we don't pay our tithes, we are robbing God. Many try to make excuses about paying tithes because Biblical times may be a little different from our current customs or because they have unique situations such as being unemployed, receiving Disability Income, Social Security, Pensions, or Retirement, etc. Unemployed people can tithe ten percent (10%) of their time volunteering or spending extra time (i.e., 24 hours=2.4 hours or 144 minutes) in God's Word or His presence or serving those in need of service who may be willing to pay, which could generate some income. People who are receiving Disability Income, Social Security, Pensions, or Retirement, etc. may still pay their tithes to honor God. Giving and paying tithes is a personal decision between you and God and no one can force you. Take a lesson from the widow in (Mark 12:41-43).

F⁵ = Finances: God Blesses Our Finances
How are We Blessed in Our Finances?

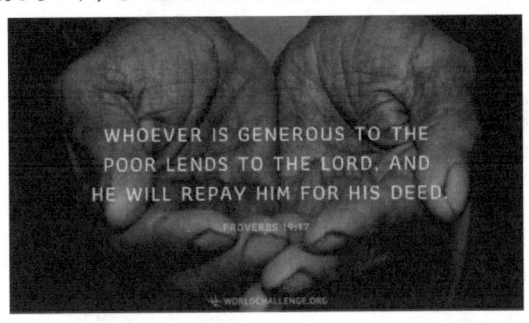

There are a variety of verses in the Bible about helping the poor but this one has always caught my attention.

Jesus told the disciples that the poor would always be among us (Matthew 26:11a) which means we will always have opportunities to give to the poor. In (Proverbs 22:9), we are told: "Blessed are those who are generous, because they feed the poor." Jesus also told the disciples that when we help those in need, it is like helping Him. (Matthew 25:31-40) To make it plain, we should treat others the same way we would treat Jesus and I pray we would treat Him with kindness and dignity if He were to meet us on a street corner asking for our help. When the Holy Spirit prompt us to help others, we should not try to speculate how they arrived at their current state of neediness nor should we think about what they will do with the money or food. Even though God has chosen the poor to be rich in faith, (James 2:5) they still have physical needs to be met. Besides, we are reminded in (Acts 20:35) that it is more blessed to give than to receive.

F^5 = Finances: God Blesses Our Finances
How are We Blessed in Our Finances?

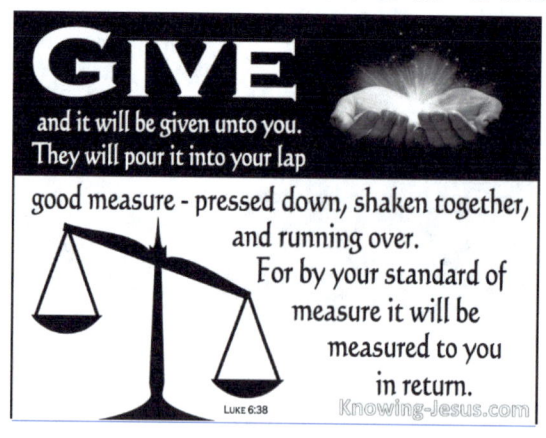

As I was preparing to commence this last chapter, the verse above was impressing upon me as the verse to begin the chapter because it has been a familiar verse in the traditional Baptist Church because it has been popular and is known as an "offering" verse. In fact, at my local church, during the offering, we used to sing a song by Ron Kenoly entitled: "Give to the Lord." Here is the link if you care to listen: https://youtu.be/3_a6sD1ywzU?si=yFB-RZWB7xzA1Bh6. I was prompted to delete the verse because it does not directly relate to giving money, however, the principle of reaping and sowing still applies in our giving. If you read (Luke 6:1-38) in its entirety, you will find that Jesus was teaching about the Sabbath, He was healing the sick, choosing the twelve disciples, giving the Beatitudes, teaching about loving your enemies and about judging others.

F^5 = Finances: God Blesses Our Finances
How are We Blessed in Our Finances?

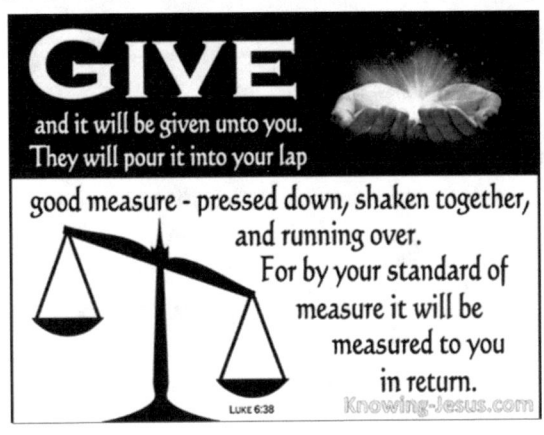

There was no mention of giving money. In the context of verses 37 and 38, Jesus is telling the disciples to stop judging and criticizing others and to forgive others or they would in turn be judged, criticized and unforgiven. Verse 38 is similar to the reaping and sowing principle found in these Bible verses: {(Job 4:8), (Psalm 126:5 KJV), and (Galatians 6:7-8)}.

Eliphaz tells us in (Job 4:8) that his experience showed that those who plant trouble and sow evil, would harvest the same.

The writer of (Psalm 126:5 KJV) tells us those who sow in tears shall reap in joy. The New Living Translation Commentary expounds upon this verse to further inform us that even our grief is not a permanent condition. Our tears can be seeds that will grow into a harvest of joy because God is able to bring good out of tragedy. (Romans 8:28)

If you find that you have been burdened by sorrow, know that your time of grief will end and you will again find joy. We must be patient as we wait for God's harvest of joy because it is coming!

Paul tells us in (Galatians 6:7-8) not to be misled into thinking that we can mock the justice of God because we will always harvest what we plant and those who sow to the flesh, will reap corruption but to those who sow to the Spirit, will harvest everlasting life from the Spirit.

F^5 = Finances: God Blesses Our Finances
How are We Blessed in Our Finances?

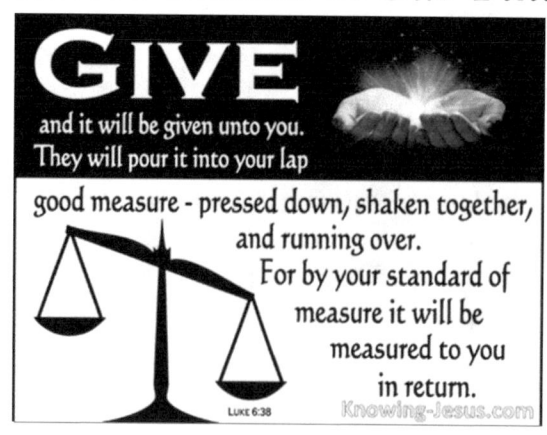

In conclusion, God allowed this verse to come up in my Bible App today and I believe He was confirming that I was to conclude with this verse and I understood why this verse is the perfect culminating verse for this book because it focuses on how we should measure the way we respond and interact in all we do in relation to our family members and friends, our motives to engage in our acts of faith, the blessings of being generous in our finances and the benefits of having fellowships with other believers and those soon to become believers!

How do you measure up in your family, with your friends, in your faith, finances and fellowships? If you find that your scale is not balanced, you may need to reevaluate these five areas of your life. I pray something has been written in this book that will help you become balanced.

Please complete the final Reflection Activity on the next page. Please pray for God's guidance (Psalm 37:23-24) and wisdom for making the necessary adjustments. (James 1:5) God bless you!

F^5 = Finances: God Blesses Our Finances
How are We Blessed in Our Finances?

Reflection Activity

1. Do you believe in the Biblical principle of tithing?
   ___ (yes) or ___ (no) Check one ☑
Explain why or why not?

_____
_____
_____

2. Have you committed to honoring God with 10% of your gross income? ___ (yes) or ___ (no) Check one ☑
Explain why or why not?

_____
_____
_____

2. Do you believe your finances will be blessed because of your commitment to pay your tithes?
   ___ (yes) or ___ (no) Check one ☑ Explain why or why not?

_____
_____
_____

~Bibliography~

I. E-sword Electronic Software, Copyright 2013

II. The Holy Bible, Old and New Testaments, Nashville, TN: Thomas Nelson, Inc., Copyright 1976

III. Life Application Study Bible, New Living Translation, Wheaton, IL: Tyndale House Publishers, Inc., Copyright (1998-1991), 1993, 1996

IV. King James Easy Reading Study Bible, New Kensington, PA: Whitaker House, Copyright 2007

V. People's Parallel Bible, New Living Translation, King James Version, Tyndale House Publishers, Inc., Carol Stream IL, Copyright 2005, 1996, 2004, 2007

VI. Images-Microsoft 365 Images, FreeBibleimages.com, and those cited on the images

VII. Merriam-Webster Dictionary and Thesaurus

VIII. Bible Gateway

IX. Book cover designed by the writer and her daughter using Google images and Canva

---

~About the Writer~
Schenida L.C. Waters is a native of Georgia and is married with two adult children, one son-in-love and one granddaughter. She enjoys spending time with family and she loves the Lord and His word, and desires to share it with the world. She enjoys singing praises to God and building up His Kingdom. She has been an educator in the public school system for twenty-seven years and is currently retired. Her prayer is that you will be blessed by this book and most of all by the Word of God.

Made in the USA
Columbia, SC
16 May 2025